VANTAGE POINT

TRANSFORM YOUR OUTLOOK
GROW YOUR FAITH
EXPERIENCE GOD ANEW

WEEKLY DEVOTIONS FROM GOD'S PERSPECTIVE

VANTAGE POINT

TRANSFORM YOUR OUTLOOK
GROW YOUR FAITH
EXPERIENCE GOD ANEW

DANIELLE L. BRIDGEFORTH

REDEMPTION
PRESS

Published by Redemption Press, PO Box 427, Enumclaw, WA 98022

Toll Free (844) 2REDEEM (273-3336)

Redemption Press is honored to present this title in partnership with the author. The views expressed or implied in this work are those of the author. Redemption Press provides our imprint seal representing design excellence, creative content, and high quality production.

Scripture quotations marked "NIV" are taken from the Holy Bible, New International Version®. NIV®. Copyright © 1984 ,1978 ,1973 by International Bible Society. Used by permission of Zondervan. All rights reserved.

Scripture quotations marked "NLT" are taken from the Holy Bible, New Living Translation, copyright © 1996. Used by permission of Tyndale House Publishers, Inc., Wheaton, IL 60189 USA. All rights reserved.

Scripture quotations marked HCSB®, are taken from the Holman Christian Standard Bible®, Copyright © 1999, 2000, 2002, 2003, 2009 by Holman Bible Publishers. Used by permission. HCSB® is a federally registered trademark of Holman Bible Publishers.

Scripture quotations marked "NRSV" Revised Standard Version of the Bible, copyright © 1946, 1952, and 1971 National Council of the Churches of Christ in the United States of America. Used by permission. All rights reserved.

Scripture quotations marked "NKJV" are taken from the New King James Version. Copyright © 1982 by Thomas Nelson, Inc. Used by permission. All rights reserved.

Scripture quotations marked "NCV" are taken from the New Century Version®. Copyright © 2005 by Thomas Nelson. Used by permission. All rights reserved.

Scripture quotations marked "ESV" are taken from The Holy Bible, English Standard Version. Copyright © 2000; 2001 by Crossway Bibles, a division of Good News Publishers. Used by permission. All rights reserved.

Scripture quotations marked "MSG" are taken from THE MESSAGE. Copyright © by Eugene H. Peterson 1993, 1994, 1995, 1996, 2000, 2001, 2002. Used by permission of NavPress Publishing Group.

Scripture quotations marked "AMP"are taken from the Amplified® Bible (AMP), Copyright © 2015 by The Lockman Foundation Used by permission. www.Lockman.org

Scripture quotations marked "TLB" are taken from The Living Bible copyright © 1971 by Tyndale House Foundation. Used by permission of Tyndale House Publishers Inc., Carol Stream, Illinois 60188. All rights reserved. The Living Bible, TLB, and the The Living Bible logo are registered trademarks of Tyndale House Publishers.

Scripture quotations marked "KJV" are from the King James Version.

Scripture quotations marked "GW" are taken from GOD'S WORD TRANSLATION. GOD'S WORD is a copyrighted work of God's Word to the Nations. Quotations are used by permission.

Scripture quotations marked "WNT" are from the Weymouth New Testament.

Scripture quotations marked NASB are taken from The New American Standard Bible , Copyright © 1960, 1962, 1963, 1968, 1971, 1972, 1973, 1975, 1977, 1995, by the Lockman Foundation. Used by permission.

ISBN 13: 978-1-68314-637-7 (Paperback)
     978-1-68314-638-4 (ePub)
     978-1-68314-639-1 (Mobi)

Library of Congress Catalog Card Number:

Why Read Vantage Point Devotional:

This book is a tool that will help draw you into a closer, more intimate walk with God. The one thing that will immediately and profoundly transform your life is to establish, maintain, and strengthen your relationship with God by calling on the name of Jesus for salvation and coming to know Jesus Christ more deeply.

Reading this devotional will give you that opportunity, and will also help you do the following:

Transform your outlook—Be open to thinking differently about God, the Bible, yourself, your life, and the spiritual principles and disciplines that should govern the way you live.

Grow your faith—Allow the Holy Spirit to develop and mature your faith through the rigor of reading, studying, meditating upon, memorizing, and applying biblical principles and promises to your life each day.

Experience God anew—Whether you are a new believer in Christ, have a seasoned faith-walk, or are simply curious and inquisitive about God and what it means to believe in Jesus—you can have a new experience and be made better by reading this devotional.

The journey of walking closely with God is dynamic and life-changing. You cannot be in a developing relationship with God and stay the same. Change—for the better—is inevitable. The quality and nature of our change is determined by how much time and energy we invest in the relationship. I have come to believe that the best person I will ever be and the greatest things I will ever do in life will flow from my experiences of simply being with and knowing Christ.

Oftentimes we either do not take the time to establish a meaningful relationship with God or we allow our relationship to remain underdeveloped because we do not understand the significance of having quality personal devotion time, i.e., spending time daily studying God's Word, and in prayer and meditation. We must spend this time with God, so that we can know God and come to recognize God's voice. We will not be able to *do* great exploits for a God that we do not *know*. Conversely, once we come to know God, learn to hear God's voice, and choose to follow Christ's example of living, then we will be able to do more with our lives than we ever dreamed or imagined. **Being precedes doing.**

The devotions contained in this book have been bathed in prayer. These devotions are intended to reveal the worth, will, wonder, and ways of God to you to spark interest and cultivate intimacy and commitment to the God being revealed. Read this devotional if you desire to develop and deepen your relationship with God. Read this devotional if you are curious about who God is and what a relationship with Jesus Christ could mean for your life. If you are open, honest, diligent, sincere, and disciplined in your approach to reading this devotional, it can become an integral part of your spiritual growth and development.

How Vantage Point Devotional Is Organized:

This book is purposely organized, easy to read, and practical. It is divided into twenty weeks and each week focuses upon one spiritual principle or theme. Each week contains the following elements:

Day 1—Introduction to the Spiritual Principle of the Week. High-level overview of the topic. I will ask you questions intended to challenge your thinking about the subject.

Day 2—Let's Go a Little Deeper. We focus on what the Bible says about the topic, review the essential scriptural and spiritual foundations, and think about how it applies to our lives.

Day 3—What Does It Mean to You? All of us have learned from our experiences. I invite you to reflect and journal about a time when you have personally dealt with the spiritual principle we are studying. We close with Bible verses to meditate on.

Day 4—Biblical Character's Perspective. Look at a character from the Bible, who exemplifies or dealt with the week's spiritual principle. Consider what we can learn from their life.

Days 5–7—Making the Connection. Moving Forward. The spiritual principle is summarized. Practical takeaways from the week's study are given.

Each of these elements will help to add depth and definition to the spiritual principle we are extracting from the biblical texts. The layering of elements is intended to strengthen your personal walk with Christ and bring you into the presence of the Lord each day.

Vantage Point is intended to be read along with the Holy Bible, not as a replacement for it. Power, strength, wisdom, and grace will flow into your life as you make daily reading of the Bible a priority. This book is a tool to make that experience more impactful. Reading the Bible and this devotional together presents a perfect opportunity for growth and spiritual development. Taken together, the devotional and the Bible will help you to better see yourself, your life, and your circumstances from God's perspective.

There are many versions of the Bible used throughout this devotional. They include: New International Version (NIV), New Living Translation (NLT), Holman Christian Standard Bible (HCSB), New Revised Standard Version (NRSV), New King James Version (NKJV), New Century Version (NCV), Message Bible (MSG), Amplified Version (AMP), J.B. Phillips New Testament (Phillips NT), The Living Bible (TLB), King James Version (KJV), God's Word (GW), Weymouth New Testament (WNT), and New American Standard Bible (NASB).

Suggested Devotional Plan: Thirty Minutes Each Day

Setting your focus and opening prayer (five minutes)

Reading of devotional passage and biblical text(s) (fifteen minutes)

Quiet reflection and listening for God's voice (five minutes)

Journaling (what did you hear?) and closing prayer (five minutes)

Questions to Consider During Your Devotional Time:

What is God saying through this passage?

How am I already doing this? How can I do this better?

What ways of thinking do I need to change based upon my study today?

What behavior(s) do I need to start, stop, or modify based upon my study today?

With whom do I need to share the lessons that I have heard today?

With Gratitude . . .

All things come of Thee, Oh Lord, I know that this is true.
So, praise and uplift Your name, I have come to do!

These words I write, but really, I want to scream!
I am so very delighted, that I have accomplished my dream.

Completing this book was indeed a great test.
Yet, all along the journey, I must say, I have been blessed.

Doubts, delays, and disappointments are just some;
Of the obstacles and setbacks that I have overcome.

Nevertheless, I made it! Lord, it is because of You.
And many have helped, supported, and encouraged me too.

You already know that I cannot call each and every name.
Yet my love and appreciation are there just the same.

You know who you are, and I thank you for wishing me well.
Thank you for praying, investing, being positive, and lifting me up when I fell.

Thank you, Mom, for loving and believing in me.
You are my most treasured blessing in this life, as all can clearly see.

Thanks, AB, for being the best brother and a cherished friend.
I appreciate you more than words can say—my love for you has no end.

Dad, I am grateful for your love and all the ways that you've stood by my side.
Colin, thank you for your support and care, my appreciation I cannot hide.

To my family–Brown, Bridgeforth, Cain, Wilson, and Benjamin, too.
You have nurtured, loved, and supported me like only family can do–Thank you!

To my extended family, church families, Pastor, mentors, and dear friends;
Your kindness is valued and I thank you for being those upon whom I can depend.

Ms. Dena and Rachel thank you for reading my words and for editing, too!
You both gave your time, expertise, and love and I appreciate you.

DreamGirls, along this journey you two have had my front, side, and back.
Thanks for helping, inspiring, praying, and for keeping me on track!

To all my Alpha Kappa Alpha sisters, from JMU up to this very day;
Thank you for hearts that are loyal and true is all that I can say!

I honor the lives and legacies of my ancestors and elders–past and present–too.
I freely admit that I would not be who or where I am, if not for you.

Vantage Point is quite simply my answer to God's call.
And I sincerely thank you for reading–thank you one and all.

Table of Contents

Week 1–Intimacy with God

Have You Seen God?

Week 1–Intimacy with God
Have You Seen God?

I had heard rumors about You but now my eyes have seen You.
(Job 42:5 HCSB)

There are fundamental and profound things that God wants to teach you about God and about yourself, hidden well beyond what the natural eyes can see. Knowing this, you cannot be satisfied with merely hearing about Christ, basing your belief (or lack thereof) upon rumors, innuendo, and conjecture. No, you must make it a point to see and know for yourself. Get to know the One who loves you too much to leave you without salvation; the One who came in human flesh to show you how to be the very best that you could ever be.

You will be *amazed* at what you can learn about God once you truly take the time to look. Too many times, we are negligent in our spiritual walks because we fail to search deeply for the meaning and purpose of our circumstances; instead, we come to the easiest conclusions regarding who God is and what God is doing in our lives. True growth and maturity, however, require that we not settle for what lies on or just beneath the surface. God is deeper, wider, stronger, wiser, and more intentional than we could ever fathom. Nevertheless, God wants us to know God and to understand God's ways. This knowledge can only be obtained as a return on our investment of time and energy into being with God, reading the Bible, and reflecting upon the way—the attitudes, behaviors, and methods—of Christ.

The very point of your current season may be to develop your eyes of faith to be able to see what is not readily visible. So the question, "Have you seen God?" is not asking you to consider what you know intellectually or even naturally about God; but rather, what you know about God because you have looked at God with the eyes of your faith.

Consider this: anyone—even an unbeliever—can observe God with their logic, intellect, and physical eyes. In fact, God does some things, which require little to no faith to be seen, simply to get humanity's attention. (See Psalm 19:1–4) Nevertheless, knowledge about the depth and essence of who God is only comes to us by and through faith. This week let us consider ways to sharpen our eyes of faith, so that we can behold God anew.

Questions to consider: What do you want to see or know about God? What current situation or relationship can you reconsider with the eyes of your faith so that you can truly see God in the midst of it?

Day 2–Let's Go a Little Deeper

Jesus says the following in the biblical passage known as the Sermon on the Mount: "Blessed are the pure in heart: *for they shall see God.*" (Matthew 5:8 KJV, emphasis added) As used in this verse, the word "pure" in the Greek means to clean or clear. This suggests that those who will actually see God must have hearts that are clean or clear from impediments and pollutants. There are many things that can clutter our hearts and thus block our view of God; things such as fear, jealously, pride, selfishness, anger, and sin. When these things are present in our hearts, they make it impossible for us to truly see who God is and to recognize when God is at work in our lives, relationships, and circumstances.

So, what about you? Is anything blocking your view of God? Perhaps it is not that something negative is cluttering your heart, maybe you are simply not alert and attentive to the movement of God in your life? Are you tired, distracted, or overwhelmed by people or predicaments? These can also have a detrimental impact upon our ability to see God.

We can establish a habit of seeing (or not seeing) God with the pattern of our lives. When you take the time and make space to become aware of God's voice, you put yourself in position to see, hear, and understand God. When you neglect to do this the opposite becomes true. You cannot see a God that you do not want to see, no matter how evident God's actions and exploits may be. If we do not want to see God, if we are not open and willing to recognize that God is always working on our behalf, we will either mistake the actions of the enemy for God, or simply miss God altogether.

Today, survey and assess the condition of your heart, as well as the pattern of your life. Be still and quiet in God's presence. Be honest with yourself. Are you cultivating a lifestyle in which God can be clearly seen, by you and by others? Sometimes, God moves in ways that are obvious and overt to us. At other times, God's moves are more covert and undercover. In either case, God acts in accordance with God's character and consistently with God's nature.

God's nature is eternal. (See Psalm 90:2) God's nature is loving. (See 1 John 4:8) God's character is honest, truthful, and good. (See James 1:17) God always gives us glimpses and insight into who God is and where God is working. All we must do is take the time and invest the energy to look, to see, and to obey.

God said, 'I will make my Goodness pass right in front of you; I'll call out the name, God, right before you. I'll treat well whomever I want to treat well and I'll be kind to whomever I want to be kind.' (Exodus 33:19 MSG)

Day 3–Learning from Our Experiences

Recall and reflect or journal about a time when you know you saw God. How did it feel to see God clearly working and moving in your life? What did you learn about God's character through that experience? How does that knowledge impact your life?

Meditate upon the following verses while asking God to show you if there is anything cluttering your heart and making it hard for you to see, trust, and obey Jesus Christ. If there is, ask God to show you what practical steps to take to clean and purify your heart and for the strength to keep your heart clear so that you can continually see God better and better.

Psalm 24:3–4: Who may ascend into the hill of the LORD? Or who may stand in his holy place? He who has clean hands and a **pure heart**; who has not lifted up his soul to an idol, nor sworn deceitfully. (NKJV, emphasis added)

Psalm 51:10: Create in me a clean heart, O God; and renew a right, persevering, and steadfast spirit within me. (AMP)

Day 4–Biblical Character Reflection: Job

Job's story is perhaps one of the most well-known in the Bible. Job was righteous. He was committed and he loved God. Nevertheless, Job experienced great tragedy and much loss in his life. In this week's reference text, Job says: "I had heard rumors about You, but now my eyes have seen You." (Job 42:5 HCSB) Job helps us to understand that sometimes we come to see God more clearly after we have had to experience storms and dark times. Job thought he knew God, but life taught him that he had a lot more to learn about who God is and how and why God acts. Interestingly, before Job experienced his hard times and difficulty, he had fear in his heart, which most likely had obstructed his ability to see God.

Look at what Job said, "For the thing I feared has overtaken me, and what I dreaded has happened to me. I cannot relax or be still; I have no rest, for trouble comes." (Job 3:25–26 HCSB) Even though Job was righteous, faithful, and rich, he still had fear deep within his heart and dread plagued his mind. Because of this, he was not able to see that God was present and well able to take care of him. He lacked peace because his view of God was being

impeded. Ultimately, Job received exactly what he had antici[
and feared.

Job shows us the importance of driving pollutants out of our hearts. Things like sin, fear, jealously, un-forgiveness, and shame lie in wait for the best opportunity to rear their ugly heads. Do not give these things a chance. Purify your heart so that nothing prohibits you from truly seeing God and walking in the power of the Holy Spirit.

What else stands out to you from Job's story? What other biblical character or real-life person inspires you on the topic of purifying your heart so that you can better see God?

Days 5-7–Making the Connection. Moving Forward.

Purifying your heart will have a great impact upon your quality of life. Our heart is the place where everything comes together. Our thoughts, our desires, our dreams, our memories, our pains, and our triumphs are all in our heart. Our heart is soft and sensitive and yet very resilient. Our heart retains and remembers and yet it knows very well how to release and forget. Next to your spirit, your heart is the one aspect of yourself to which you should pay the most attention.

Consider what the writer says in Proverbs, "Guard your heart above all else, for it determines the course of your life." (4:23 NLT) In other words, the condition of your heart impacts the course and direction of your very life. Do not neglect your heart because doing so will be detrimental to every aspect of your life.

This week we have focused upon creating the right conditions in our heart so that we can clearly see God. Let us move on from here, being diligent to guard and protect our heart from all that would pollute and contaminate it. Here are some practical steps to take to protect your heart. Over the next few days, meditate and reflect upon how to apply these steps in your life.

Pray and repent often. Unresolved issues of sin will cause our heart to become hardened. To guard against this, practice repentance regularly. Even if you cannot recall anything that you did to disappoint God, make it your practice to ask God to cleanse your heart; it can be as simple as praying this prayer: "Create in me a clean heart, O God, and renew a right spirit within me." (Psalm 51:10 ESV) We sin willfully, stupidly, and sometimes just negligently. But, no matter what type of sin it is, it must be dealt with or we give it power to clutter our heart and block the flow of grace, mercy, peace, and love in and out of our lives.

Protect the gateways to your heart. Our eyes, ears, and minds are the gateways to our heart. If we want to keep our heart clean, we must be careful to protect what we let in through these gateways. The more we grow in Christ, the more sensitive we will become to stuff that can pollute our lives. Gossip, pornography, negativity, greed, or any of the "works of the flesh" found in Galatians 5:19–21 must be curtailed. Dwell on what is true, honest, just, pure, lovely, of good report, virtuous, and praiseworthy. (See Philippians 4:8) Align yourself with people who will help you to stay focused on God and the things of God. There is way too much riding on the condition of your heart for you to be casual and inattentive to its condition. And, remember what goes into your heart will eventually come out. Be vigilant to make sure that everything that flows from your life is pleasing to God.

Practice praise. Joy, gratitude, and worship have a way of washing our heart of all that seeks to clutter it. When we are in a posture of praise, anything that is not God-honoring and God-edifying will be driven out of our heart. Be more deliberate about giving thanks and praise to God. Learn new songs, write Jesus thank-you notes, or just meditate on God's goodness daily. Whatever you do, do not let bitterness, ingratitude, discontentment, and pride set in. Keep your heart pure so that you can have a clear sight line to God.

Let the words of my mouth and the meditation of my heart be acceptable in Your sight, O Lord, my strength and my Redeemer. (Psalm 19:14 NKJV)

Week 2–Praise

The Choice Is Yours; Choose Praise!

Week 2–Praise
The Choice Is Yours; Choose Praise!

I WILL bless the Lord at all times; His praise SHALL continually be in my mouth. My life MAKES its boast in the Lord; let the humble and afflicted hear and BE GLAD. (Psalm 34:1–2 AMP, emphasis added)

We must make the choice to praise and honor God with our words and with our very lives. Circumstances may impact your ability to do many things in this life, but giving glory to God is not one of them; that choice is yours. Come hell or high water, come victory or defeat, each of us must make up in our mind and heart that "I WILL bless the Lord." We must decide that we will magnify the God who created us, the Savior, Jesus Christ, who died for us, and the Holy Spirit who secures and keeps us each moment of every day. Choose to praise! And then, invite others to join you.

You see, once you have decided what the pattern of your life will be, you are prepared to have the right response when crises, tragedies, and triumphs arise. They will all surely come. When they do, will you handle life? Or will life handle you? The inherent power of praise in our lives is that it serves as an instant reminder of at least two important truths. First, praise reminds us that we are not alone. Whenever we are having a difficult time, we generally feel alone and that makes us discouraged. Praise shifts our focus away from our feelings of separation, isolation, and fear and toward the truth that God IS. When we praise we can remember that despite our current circumstances, Christ promises to never abandon us. (See Matthew 28:20)

Second, praise reminds us of God's perfect ability to help us. Once we recall that God is present with us, then we are reminded that God is always able to help us. There is no lack, insufficiency, or weakness in God. God is always able to overpower, overcome, outlast, and outmaneuver anyone or anything that opposes us. Moreover, God is always willing to help you. Praise is a perfect way to pause and reflect upon the goodness and able-ness of God. When you praise you divert your attention from what you cannot do, to what God is more than able to accomplish in and through your life. This week let us get some training on praise so that we can see its power at work in our lives.

Questions to consider: What is your definition of praise? How do you praise? Does everyone praise God the same way? Is intentional praise a regular aspect of your life and relationship with God?

Day 2–Let's Go a Little Deeper

Praise is often misunderstood and therefore its power is not completely unleashed in our lives. Praise can be done anyplace and at any time. When we praise we essentially do three things. We acknowledge, we acclaim, and we anticipate.

When we acknowledge, it means that we recognize and affirm that God is worthy of praise and adoration at all times. We know from our human relationships that simply acknowledging someone's contribution, presence, and support goes a long way. Consider what it would mean to practice this principle in your relationship with God. It would have a great impact upon your outlook and perspective, if you would continually acknowledge the presence, power, provision, and protection of God in your life.

To acclaim means to be strong and emphatic in our praise; to applaud. This has to do with the enthusiasm with which we praise God. Sometimes, praise can become so routine and devoid of feeling. This ought not to be so. Our praise to God should always be thunderous, even if only in our hearts. This is not to suggest that we must always be outwardly expressive in our praise; for moments of quiet, reflective, and contemplative praise are certainly necessary. Nevertheless, let us not forget that praise is more than merely bringing our hands together to make noise. Praise is our life's response to the attributes and actions of God. Thus, praise should be inwardly and outwardly boisterous.

To anticipate means to have an expectation that something will happen before it does. Our praise to God should be anticipatory. We praise God for what God has done *and* we praise God for what we expect God to do in the future. When we anticipate, we do not need the final confirmation or manifestation of certain "facts" before we act. But rather, our faith in God's character compels us to give God due praise, even in advance. The truth of the matter is that even if God does not do anything else for us, we still owe God praise. So, to give praise for what we anticipate is just to recognize that God is still God and still able to do God-sized things in and through our lives.

Today make the decision to begin incorporating these three aspects of praise into your daily worship practice. Moreover, diversify your praise by utilizing the following five postures when you praise: Raising your hands   Speaking with your mouth   Standing in honor
Bowing in submission   Revering in silence

For great is the Lord, and greatly to be praised; he is to be revered above all gods. (1 Chronicles 16:25 NRSV)

Day 3–Learning from Our Experiences

Recall and reflect or journal about a significant experience you have had praising God. Do you recall the first time you praised in a new or different way (i.e., dancing, lifting of hands, speaking out loud)? How did that experience make you feel?

Meditate upon the following verse while asking God to give you new insight about why God is worthy of your praise. What ways can you encourage or inspire others to praise God along with you?

Psalm 34:3: Oh, magnify the Lord with me, and let us exalt His name together. (NKJV)

Day 4—Biblical Character Reflection: David

David danced before the LORD with all his might.... (2 Samuel 6:14a NRSV)

David is attributed with writing most of the book of Psalms. At his heart, he was a man of praise. He praised God wherever he was. He praised God in every circumstance. He praised God no matter who was watching him. David made the choice to praise God with his life. David's life shows us that when praise is a regular and consistent aspect of our relationship with God, our current predicaments and circumstances will not be able to stop it.

David did not always enjoy an easy journey. He was often in trouble and under attack. He knew disappointment and pain. Nevertheless, no matter what he may have been experiencing, David knew from where his strength came—his source was his Lord. (See 1 Samuel 30:6) As we reflect upon the praise example lived by David, consider your own life. Where do you turn in times of difficulty, distress, and disappointment? Be honest with yourself about whether praise flows naturally from your life in each season or if you are only able to praise when things are going well. This is not a time to feel guilty; this is a time to be honest about where you are. If you currently do not have a pattern of praise in your life, you can learn from King David.

There are at least two things that David did, which helped him to establish a pattern of praise in his life. The first thing is that David rehearsed what he knew about the Lord over and over again. David remained in a posture of praise because he never let the character and exploits of God get too far away from his mind and mouth. We can stand to set aside time daily simply to consider who God is and what God has done. If we establish this pattern, especially during times of peace and ease, it will be more likely that these truths will flood our hearts and minds during our times of trouble.

The second thing that David did was to write down his recollections and beliefs about the Lord. Today, we can look to the Bible to see what David experienced with God. Where do you look when you need to be reminded about what God has done for you? Each of us keeps some memories hidden deep within our hearts, but the fact is that memory can fail us. It is one thing to look to the Bible and read about David's experiences with God; it is another thing entirely to establish and maintain our own track record with God.

If you are not already doing so, start a journal of gratitude, praise reports, memories, and prayers. This record will become your own book of Psalms. As you think about the goodness of God and make a record of those thoughts, it will be easier for you to praise God in every circumstance.

Praise the LORD, O my soul, and forget not all his benefits. (Psalm 103:2 NIV)

Days 5-7—Making the Connection. Moving Forward.

The choice to praise God continuously is one which we all should make. Life has a way of depleting us and one of the sure ways to replenish our energy, our joy, and our faith is through our praise. Praise is a weapon that is appropriate to use in every circumstance. Praise keeps us focused upon the truth, even when we are being bombarded with lies and falsities about ourselves and about our God.

This week we have studied what praise is, why it is important, and discussed some of its inherent benefits. So, how will you make praise a more consistent and prominent aspect of your faith-walk moving forward? Here are a few suggestions:

1. Incorporate new "praise postures/movements" into your daily and weekly regimen. Begin to display praise to God by adding these new practices to your life pattern. For example, try lifting your hands, saying hallelujah, clapping, or singing.

During times of corporate and private worship, doing these practices will help you take your focus off you and place it onto God. It may be awkward at first, but as you keep at it, it will become more natural.

2. Keep a daily, weekly, or monthly record of your experiences with God. This can be kept by hand or electronically. Begin to write your own book of Psalms which tells of your beliefs about and experiences with Jesus Christ. Do not merely keep a record, however. Take the time periodically to read and reflect upon what you have learned and experienced with God. This practice will become a great source of encouragement and strength as your record with God grows.

3. Put together a praise playlist which will keep your heart and mind attuned to Christ no matter what may be going on in your life. Choose music from different genres and by various artists. Have a wide range of lyrics and tempos. Remember praise is a lifestyle, so these songs should encompass every area of your living. Have fun with it! And remember to share your favorite playlists with others.

Week 3–Generosity
The Enriching Power of Generosity

Week 3–Generosity
The Enriching Power of Generosity

Give and you will receive. Your gift will return to you in full—pressed down, shaken together to make room for more, running over, and poured into your lap. The amount you give will determine the amount you get back. (Luke 6:38 NLT)

It is often hard to visualize this truth: the richest among us are those who generously share what they have. We simply cannot get more by hoarding and saving all that we have. The only way to *get* is to *give*.

This is not only a financial principle. Generosity is a lifestyle. Generosity stems from the heart, not merely from our wallet and bank accounts. Generosity should encompass every area of your life and living. And, if you want to expand your influence, and/or strengthen any presumed area of weakness in your life, you should become more generous. Survey your entire life and existence. What is it that you think you lack? Is it love? Time? Peace? Patience? Joy? Happiness? Laughter? Understanding? Whatever it is, dare to start giving that very thing to others—even those who are seemingly undeserving. As you do so, you will come to find that being generous has a way of enriching not only the receiver, but also the giver.

The torment, pain, violence, ugliness, and despair which we often see played out on our television screens is simply a result of our failure as a nation to put generosity fully into practice. Violence cannot create peace. Un-forgiveness cannot give birth to love. Hatred will not bring unity. Oppression will not lead to freedom. We must sow what we eventually want to reap. Or, we will keep reaping what we have already sown. Indeed, the Bible is clear, "Remember this: Whoever sows sparingly will also reap sparingly, and whoever sows generously will also reap generously." (2 Corinthians 9:6 NIV)

The challenge is for us to follow the model of Jesus Christ—for while humanity was lost in our sin (disconnected, unloving, and unlovable)—Christ died for us all. (See Romans 5:6–8) Thankfully, God did not wait for us to deserve salvation before God sent Jesus to save us. No, God thought we were worth saving, even when we looked unredeemable. We cannot afford to delay either. There is an enriching power in generosity. The question is: Will you trust God enough to manifest this power in your life? This week we will uncover some keys to unleashing the enriching power of generosity.

One person gives freely, yet gains more; another withholds what is right, only to become poor. A generous person will be enriched, and the one who gives a drink of water will receive water. (Proverbs 11:24–25 HCSB)

Questions to consider: What is your definition of generosity? In which areas of your life are you most generous? In which areas of your life do you find it difficult to give? Are there certain people to whom it is hard for you to be generous? Why is this?

Day 2–Let's Go a Little Deeper

Already you are well to the fore in every good quality - you have faith, you can express that faith in words; you have knowledge, enthusiasm and your love for us. Could you not add generosity to your virtues? (2 Corinthians 8:7 Phillips NT)

Have you ever considered that generosity is a virtue? There is grace in generosity. When we are operating under this grace, our giving will take on certain distinct characteristics. We will be able to give (in all areas) in ways that would not be possible or even thought about in our own strength. But, with God working in us, we will not only give, but our giving will also inspire and motivate others to do the same. We have all seen people operating under the grace of generosity. We recognize them because they give freely, without complaint, and with no regard for what they will get in return. Their generosity manifests itself as commitment, loyalty, and even love. This type of giving is prompted by God and sustained by the power of the Holy Spirit.

It is critical, however, that we understand the distinction between being generous and simply giving. The key is our attitude and the reason behind the gift. When we have the grace of generosity, it will be our pleasure to give. Anyone can give, but giving with an attitude of smugness or meanness, or for self-serving reasons does not honor God.

In 2 Corinthians 8:1–7, the apostle Paul uses a testimony about the generosity of the Macedonia churches to inspire and encourage the church at Corinth to grow in this area of generosity. This passage helps us to understand how to unleash the grace of generosity in our lives as well. The first step is to do what the Macedonians did: give ourselves to the Lord. (See verse 5) This is where it starts. The idea of operating under the grace of generosity cannot be fulfilled without our being connected to the Lord, who is the Source of all generosity and grace.

God is our perfect example of generosity. God freely gives everything to those whom God knows cannot repay. God gives above and beyond what is expected or anticipated. God gives to us even though we do not deserve it. Of all the reasons we say we *cannot* give, God overlooks and gives to us anyway. This is generosity.

When you give yourself to the Lord first and foremost, you will find that "God is working in you, giving you the desire and the power to do what pleases [God]." (Philippians 2:13 NLT) We cannot access the grace of generosity unless or until we give ourselves fully to God, through a relationship with the Son, Jesus Christ. Once we do this, God will give us the power, wisdom, courage, strength, and peace to live generously.

Today, consider how you can more fully give yourself to the Lord. Are there areas where you are not allowing God complete access? Have you decided that you will not open your heart or mind to God regarding certain issues? Consider this, God has already assigned people and circumstances to your life in which God wants you to be generous. However, you will not be able to recognize these opportunities and respond unless you are completely devoted to Jesus Christ. Give yourself to God and then you will find that it is much easier to release whatever God has put into your hands.

Day 3–Learning from Our Experiences

Recall and reflect or journal about a time when: (1) you were the recipient of someone's act of generosity and (2) you were generous toward another person at the prompting of God. Do not limit yourself to examples of only material giving. How did those experiences make you feel?

Meditate upon the following verse. Consider how generous God has been to you. Pray for God to cultivate a heart of generosity within you.

James 1:17: Every generous act and every perfect gift is from above, coming down from the Father of lights; with Him there is no variation or shadow cast by turning. (HCSB)

Day 4–Biblical Character Reflection: Ruth

Ruth is a great example of one who lived generously. Ruth exemplifies what it looks like when the grace of generosity is operating in and through our lives. Ruth's story is told in four brief chapters in the Old Testament book bearing her name.

Ruth was a young, widowed Moabite woman. After her husband died, she chose to go with her mother-in-law, Naomi, to the land of Judah (a foreign land), instead of going to her own country with her own family and kindred. The sensible and expected thing for Ruth to do after staying with her mother-in-law for ten years after her husband's death, was to look out for herself. Nevertheless, Ruth generously remained loyal and committed to Naomi, even though Naomi tried hard to persuade her to do otherwise. Ruth did not merely think about herself. She had more on her mind than finding a new husband and bearing children. Ruth was generous, and it was seemingly to her own detriment because of the unlikeliness that she would marry again or have children, if she went to Judah. The fact that Ruth gave so sacrificially is evidence that the grace of God was flowing in her life.

There are a couple of important principles we can glean from Ruth's story. The first is that there is power in living a righteous life. Naomi knew the Lord, and even though life had been bitter and unfair to her (her husband and two sons died in a ten-year period), she still had deep faith. Her faith convinced Ruth to abandon her own god and become committed to Naomi's God. Naomi most likely did not realize the impact that her faith was having upon her daughter-in-law. At the right time, however, Naomi witnessed Ruth's confession of faith to a new God—the God which Ruth had come to know by watching the life of her mother-in-law.

The second thing we learn through Ruth's story is that generosity is ultimately rewarded by God. God rewarded Ruth for her generous and sacrificial love to Naomi. Ruth eventually remarried to a godly man and she bore a son who was in the birth line of Jesus, Israel's promised Messiah. Ruth's generosity enriched many lives, including her own. Her future husband Boaz even boasted about how well-known her acts of generosity were:

> Boaz answered her, "Everything you have done for your mother-in-law since your husband's death has been fully reported to me: [how] you left your father and mother and the land of your birth, and [how] you came to a people you didn't previously know. *May the LORD reward you for what you have done, and may you receive a full reward from the LORD God of Israel, under whose wings you have come for refuge.*" (Ruth 2:11–12 HCSB, emphasis added)

Ruth's story shows us that God always honors those who live truly generous lives—lives characterized by selflessness, kindness, loyalty, and grace. Take the time to read Ruth's story. What two or three characteristics can you take from her life and add to strengthen your own life?

Days 5-7—Making the Connection. Moving Forward.

Earlier this week, we referenced 2 Corinthians 8:1–7. In this passage, Paul is talking to the church at Corinth about his desire for them to develop the grace of generosity. As we discussed, the first step to unleashing this power is to give ourselves fully and freely to the Lord. Only when the Spirit of God is working in us, can we live generously.

The second step to cultivating the grace of generosity is taking advantage of the opportunities God gives us to act generously. God often presents us with chances to be generous to others. We must recognize and act upon them. You can know that you are operating under the grace of generosity when your giving, in every area of your life, has these four characteristics:

Your giving is unrestrained. Take the limits off. This does not necessarily mean that we are to blindly give without regard for our means and responsibilities. God does call us to be good stewards over all that has been assigned to our hands. Instead, unrestrained giving means that our resources are never an excuse for why we cannot be generous. There are times when God simply wants to know if we are willing; if so, God will make us able. When faced with an opportunity to give, consider what you *can* do and not merely what you cannot do.

Your giving is unforced. Give freely and voluntarily. We know we have the grace of generosity when we do not wait to be asked, but we willingly give what is needed or desired. We should freely give as we have freely received. We help others to see God better when we allow God to give through us. Pray for wisdom, insight, open eyes, and a heart to be able to recognize the needs around you.

Then, willingly give to meet and even exceed the need. Remember, "[God] will make you rich in every way so that you can always give freely. And your giving . . . will cause many to give thanks to God." (2 Corinthians 9:11 NCV)

Your giving has a sense of urgency. Do not delay in your giving. When you become aware of a need, you should see about it urgently. In the day and times in which we live, we see so much need and lack all around us that we can become desensitized to it. We can become more concerned about how and why someone is in need than we are about actually meeting the need. Do not be nonchalant about the various needs of others. Purpose in your heart to give and then do so quickly and cheerfully. (See 2 Corinthians 9:7)

Your giving is unexpected. Give in a way that refreshes. When we give what is unexpected, we know that we are operating in grace. This is especially true when we give to those whom we do not know, or who have no means to repay us. Nevertheless, we have the assurance that God always sees us, even when others do not. So, be obedient to the mandates in God's word about when and how to give. For, when you are, you can trust God to be faithful in bringing biblical promises to pass in your life. Here's an example of one such mandate and promise: "But when you do a kindness to someone, do it secretly—don't tell your left hand what your right hand is doing. And your Father, who knows all secrets, will reward you." (Matthew 6:3–4 TLB)

Generosity is a unique grace that God gives to those who have first completely given themselves to the Lord. Look for ways to operate in this grace. Let your sincere prayer be that God expand your capacity to be generous, not only with your money, but also with your time and your talents. Remember that you can never out give God. So, as you determine to become more generous, you are sure to experience more generosity coming back to you.

Week 4–Forgiveness
Give Forgiveness a Chance

Week 4—Forgiveness
Give Forgiveness a Chance

Make allowance for each other's faults and forgive anyone who offends you. **Remember, the Lord forgave you,** *so you must forgive others.*
(Colossians 3:13 NLT, emphasis added)

This week we are going to dissect an important topic that each of us will face many times along our journey: forgiveness. We all understand, at least mentally and theoretically, that we ought to forgive others of their wrongdoings and mistakes. Nevertheless, we often have a hard time living forgiveness on a practical level. As we go into this study, pray and ask God to give you an open mind, heart, and spirit to look at forgiveness anew, from God's perspective. We will not start our study by seeking to convince you that you should forgive; suffice it to say that it is commanded throughout the Bible. Instead, let's go directly to what makes it hard and why we struggle to live out forgiveness.

Forgiveness is hard because sometimes life really hurts. This statement needs no explanation. We all know pain. Moreover, we have all caused pain on some level. Pain is a great equalizer in life, and to forgive others for hurting us is more than a notion. The reality is that forgiveness is a process. Like the healing of most hurts, forgiveness does not happen all at once, but we must at least be open to it for it to happen at all.

Forgiveness is hard because we feel justified in holding on to the offense. Most of us do not want to play the victim, but the fact is when you have been victimized by time, people, or situations, it is not easy to let the offense go. We must understand, however, that holding on to our pains only perpetuates them. The sooner you allow God to heal you from your hurts, the sooner you can experience the goodness that God intends for your life.

Forgiveness is hard because it feels unfair. The thought of "letting someone off" (which is how many characterize forgiveness) is almost as traumatizing as the initial offense. It is especially hard to release the offense if there has never been an acknowledgment or apology by the other person. Nevertheless, retained blame and unresolved feelings about wrongs done to us are toxic. It is not fair to your quality of life to hold on to such things. The longer you hold on to the offense, the more you drag out your pain.

Notice that all three of the reasons listed above deal with how we feel about forgiveness. It is always important to acknowledge our feelings. Your feelings are valid and serve a purpose. You do not honor God, nor help yourself, by denying or repressing your feelings. One reason why forgiveness is a process is that it takes time to wade through our feelings. You should allow yourself to feel the pain and give yourself permission to articulate that pain on some level. We are not always able to talk to the perpetrator, but it is important to our healing that we express our pain, disappointment, and frustration. Feelings matter.

Nevertheless, God does not intend for us to live our lives purely based upon our feelings. No matter how valid and sincere, feelings are limited. Forgiveness is not about feelings; it is about faith. Forgiveness is about what you believe about God. To live out forgiveness requires spiritual power which only comes from being and staying connected to Christ. Our decision to forgive should be based upon God's character, not the lack of character of the one who hurt us. The basis of our forgiveness is that God has forgiven us. Indeed, God continues to offer us forgiveness for our sins and shortcomings.

Notwithstanding how appropriate forgiveness is, it is also complicated. Therefore, if we are going to do it, we must have a plan. The plan can be found in this week's focus text:

> But one thing I do: <u>Forgetting what is behind</u> and <u>straining toward what is ahead</u>, I <u>press on toward the goal</u> to win the prize for which God has called me heavenward in Christ Jesus. (Philippians 3:13b-14 NIV, emphasis added)

The key aspects of the plan are underlined above. This is what we must do if we are going to live out forgiveness. We must forget what is behind us; strain toward what is in front of us; and press on to our goal, which is God's high calling for our lives. We will deal with the steps to the plan starting tomorrow. Today, take some time to consider the questions below. Read all of Philippians 3 and begin to memorize the verses quoted above.

Questions to consider: What do you need to forget? Are you honestly more focused upon what is in front of you or what is behind you? What is God calling you to do in life?

Day 2—Let's Go a Little Deeper

Forgiveness will not just happen. Forgiveness is a deliberate decision that requires intentionality, spiritual muscle, and godly wisdom. If we do not have a plan for how to handle our hurts we will find that instead of healing from them, we will be hamstrung by them—inhibited from living the life that God has ordained. In other words, if you do not handle your hurts, your hurts will handle you. This does not need to be the case in your life because we are going to develop a plan. When it comes to forgiveness, this is what you must choose to do:

Forget the past. Admittedly this is the hardest part about forgiveness. How can we forgive that which we cannot forget? Well, the first thing to understand is that forgetting is also a process. It takes time to stop remembering and recalling the bad, wrong, deceptive, mean, unjust, and unkind things that have been done and said to us. Nevertheless, with the aid of the Holy Spirit, it is possible.

When you look up the word "forgetting" as it is used in Philippians 3:13, in the original Greek, you learn that it means to neglect or to hide. What this suggests is that if we are going to forget, we will need to push the memory to the back—out of the forefront of our mind. We cannot continue to rehearse the stories and replay the incidences of how we have been hurt and expect to forget them. At some point, you must choose to disregard the memory. Forget it; not because it did not hurt, not because it was not bad, but simply because continuing to remember keeps you in bondage.

God wants you to be free. Freedom requires that you forget. The enemy wants you to be in bondage, so those memories will keep bombarding your mind unless and until you become anchored in God's Word and establish a pattern of pushing down and back the thoughts that do not help you. It is like what Paul said in 2 Corinthians 10:4–5:

> We fight with weapons that are different from those the world uses. Our weapons have power from God that can destroy the enemy's strong places. We destroy people's arguments and every proud thing that raises itself against the knowledge of God. **We capture every thought and make it give up and obey Christ.** (NCV, emphasis added)

Forgetting will most likely not happen quickly. In fact, we may never totally forget the incident or the pain. But, we can train ourselves to remember less and less. The memory does not have to trigger the same physical or emotional response in us that it once did. You may even need to seek professional help before you can start the process of forgetting. Still, it can be done. You can take authority over your memories and do not have to keep retelling your "war stories." Learn to forget the past.

Strain forward. The process of forgetting in practice means to continuously stretch and strain to focus on something else. See, if we do not replace the empty space with something positive, eventually those old thoughts will come flooding back. There is a myriad of things which can trigger a negative or explosive memory. We can be caught off-guard in a moment and seemingly transported back to the time when we were first hurt. That is why we must strain. Exert sufficient energy to not only forget, but also to move forward. To develop a pattern of replacing bad memories, follow the admonition and encouragement which Paul gives in Philippians 4:8:

> Summing it all up, friends, I'd say you'll do best by filling your minds and meditating on things true, noble, reputable, authentic, compelling, gracious — the best, not the worst; the beautiful, not the ugly; things to praise, not things to curse. (MSG)

Straining connotes the idea of being fully engaged. We do not use our mind only, but also our heart and our mouth. You must tell yourself the truth about who you are and who God is, despite what harmful things others have done. Eventually, you will find that you have established new thought patterns and moved forward. You will find that the sting of the injury does not hurt quite as much. You may never fully forget that you were once hurt, but after time, you will find that you remember less and less.

Press toward God. The effect of straining to move forward and deliberately applying God's Word to our lives is that we will be drawn closer to God. Of course, staying close to God requires that we press. Think of pressing toward God as elevating God, God's words, and God's ways above everything else. As you press toward God you will understand that whatever the original offense was, it was only temporary. God is eternal. The promises that God offers us are permanent, and we can only grab hold of them by force. Once we have ahold of God's promises, they are ours and nothing and no one can take them from us. Forgiveness is essentially an uneven exchange. We exchange our pain, our disappointment, our frailty for the healing, sufficiency, grace, and strength that only God can provide. Do not keep hanging on to what is weighing you down. Press into God's presence and be free.

Focus on your calling. The final part of our plan to walk out forgiveness is to focus on what is better: the great call of God on your life. Be clear, where you are going is better than where you have been. Whatever opposes you is nothing in comparison to the God who is working in you and wants to work through you to change the world. Key verses to ponder are 2 Corinthians 4:17–18:

> For this slight momentary affliction is preparing us for an eternal weight of glory beyond all measure, because we look not at what can be seen but at what cannot be seen; for what can be seen is temporary, but what cannot be seen is eternal. (NRSV)

These verses are not suggesting that what you experienced and endured was insignificant, but rather that it is not worth comparing to what God has and is willing to do in your life. God has called you by name and has great plans to fulfill through you. Trust that God can redeem the time, renew every broken area, and reinvigorate every dream, so you can reclaim the life that Jesus died for you to have. Stay focused on God and stay connected to the Source of all the power that you need—Jesus Christ.

Day 3–Learning from Our Experiences

Recall and reflect or journal about a time when: (1) you had to forgive someone and (2) you needed to be forgiven by someone who you hurt. How did you feel in each circumstance? In each case, what was the most difficult part? How did you express your forgiveness? How did you respond to being forgiven?

Meditate upon the following verses. Consider how God has already forgiven you. Pray to gain a deeper understanding about how important forgiveness is to God. Ask God to cultivate a heart of forgiveness within you.

Psalm 86:5: For You, Lord, are good, and ready to forgive, and abundant in mercy to all those who call upon You. (NKJV)

1 John 1:9: If we confess our sins, [God] is faithful and just to forgive us our sins and to cleanse us from all unrighteousness. (NKJV)

Day 4–Biblical Character Reflection: Joseph

As far as I am concerned, God turned into good what you meant for evil, for He brought me to this high position I have today so that I could save the lives of many people. (Genesis 50:20 TLB)

Joseph's story is told in the last fourteen chapters of the book of Genesis (37–50). His life is a complicated tale which starts with him being the preferred and favored son of his father, Jacob. While it was not his fault that he was preferred, Joseph made his situation worse by bragging to his older brothers about having dreams in which he saw himself being elevated above them. Eventually, Joseph's brothers became so incensed that they plotted to kill him. His oldest brother, Reuben, had compassion for him and disrupted the plan to take Joseph's life. Nevertheless, Reuben could not stop the others from selling Joseph into slavery. They told Jacob that Joseph had been mauled by a wild animal all the while they knew that they had sold him off to some passersby from Egypt for twenty pieces of silver.

Fast forward approximately twenty-two years and Joseph has now been elevated by the current Pharaoh to second in command in all of Egypt. He got this position because he operated in the wisdom and favor that God had granted him, interpreting dreams and showing financial and business acumen. Now, there was a severe famine in the Land of Canaan where his family lived, but, thanks to Joseph's wisdom, there was plenty of grain in Egypt. This meant that everyone traveled from near and far seeking much-needed food, everyone including Joseph's brothers. After several meetings in which Joseph saw his brothers, though they did not recognize him, he finally revealed himself as their long-lost brother whom they had sold into slavery. They were shocked and amazed.

Eventually, Joseph moved his entire family to the land of Goshen, where his father, Jacob, subsequently died. It was not until after their father's death that Joseph's brothers became fearful that he might finally try to exact revenge against them for selling him into slavery all those years before. At the end of the story, however, Joseph walked in forgiveness. He did not punish his brothers for what they had done. Over the years, he had become convinced that even though his brothers did a terrible, unthinkable thing to him, God had worked it out for their good. God had not made them sell Joseph into slavery, but once he was there, God allowed Joseph to experience blessings, grace, and elevation.

Joseph's story is a great reminder that forgiveness is always possible when we trust and draw close to God. By staying connected to God, Joseph developed a perspective which was not based upon his painful past, but upon the goodness of God which had always awaited him in his future. Joseph knew from a young age that God had a call on his life. He never lost sight of the vision of greatness that God had given to him, not even during his most difficult days. Because Joseph was straining forward, he could see that God had superimposed God's will over that of his brothers. What they meant for evil, God turned for good! Prayerfully, we can gain this same type of perspective in our own lives.

Days 5-7–Making the Connection. Moving Forward.

In this week's study, we have laid out a plan for how we can walk out true forgiveness in our lives. We established that we forgive because God has freely forgiven us. Moreover, forgiveness takes time and we must confront, not overlook, what has been done to us. Ultimately, however, we must choose to stop looking back and strain forward.

So, where are you? Is there someone or something in your past which you need to forgive? Spend time over the next few days reviewing Joseph's story and asking God to show you how to live out forgiveness in your life as he did. Here are a few things to consider as you grapple with the decision to give forgiveness a chance.

You have the capacity to forgive. Sometimes we act as if forgiveness is something that we are required to do in our own strength. The truth is that being connected to God, through a relationship with Jesus Christ, gives us the capacity to forgive. As we learned earlier in the week, forgiveness is one of God's core characteristics. (See again Psalm 86:5 and 1 John 1:9) Our relationship with Christ gives us access to a deep reservoir of forgiveness. Since each of us is a recipient of the grace and forgiveness of God, we should see ourselves as privileged when we get a chance to express that same forgiveness to others. We can show people so much about God when we walk in forgiveness. Forgiveness is hard, but if we dig deep we will find that we have the capacity within us, namely the Holy Spirit, to walk it out.

Understand the context. It is important to consider the context in which the injury occurred. We must understand that life comes with afflictions, bumps, and bruises. Now, certainly, we should not linger in places and relationships where we are abused and devalued. Even so, we cannot "break up" with everyone who hurts us. Too often we do not realize how the circumstances with which a person was dealing at the time may have impacted how they treated us.

Stress reveals a lot. None of us are our best selves when we are in high-pressure, intense, and stressful situations, especially for prolonged periods of time. Things like death, depression, disappointment, unemployment, transition, financial distress, and the like can make us act ugly. These things are not excuses for us to act out, nevertheless they are real pressure points. Perhaps the person who hurt you was going through a difficult period at the time. Even though they hurt you, it may not have been about you at all. Get some perspective from someone who may not be as close to the situation as you are. Understanding the context may make forgiveness a little easier.

Forgiveness is a choice. To forgive or not is always a choice. This is a simple fact that we cannot get around. No matter what anyone else has done to us, we always have the power to choose how to react and respond to it. You can keep remembering the mean, hurtful things that have been said and done to you and thereby give those things and people power to control your life. Or, you can choose to forget—not ascribe any energy or power to the negative, wrongdoings of others. Pushing pain out of your mind, emotions, and life will take resolve and vigor; and ultimately, it is your choice whether you do it.

Give forgiveness a chance. Forgiveness is possible, but only if you give it a chance. You may not be able to do it. What you experienced may be too deep-seated and painful to overcome. But then again, with God's help you just may be able to let it go. You will never know until you try.

Week 5–Love
All This Love

Week 5–Love
All This Love

I give you a new command: Love one another. Just as I have loved you,
you must also love one another.   (John 13:34 HCSB)

Love is one of the most challenging concepts with which we will
ever have to grapple. Love is universal. However, each one of
us has a different understanding of love and we each give and receive love in various ways. Love is simply, complex. It is important
to every living creature. Its importance cuts across every dividing
line—be it social, cultural, economic, or political. We all need love
and we all need to give love away. Love can also be highly subjective. What it is to me and what it is to you does not have to be the
same. Love doesn't need our permission to be, yet it does require
our participation to be sustained.

Even still love, to be love, must have certain qualities and characteristics. Love must be expressed; love must be discernible to the
recipient; and love must be more concerned about its object than
the giver. The apostle Paul wrote perhaps the greatest description of
love when he penned 1 Corinthians 13. He says that love is patient
and kind, not boastful, arrogant, or rude. Love isn't pushy, irritable,
or resentful. Love does not rejoice at wrongdoing but rejoices with
the truth; love "bears all things, believes all things, hopes all things,
endures all things; love never ends." (reference to 1 Corinthians
13:4-8a HCSB) And, it is perhaps this last quality that makes love
so slippery and yet so enduring. The fact is love must abide to be
real. Love is not expected to simply visit; love is obliged to stay.

Some of us immediately doubt that statement because in the days and times in which we live, we are more likely to see what happens when there is a lack of love instead of the beauty that comes when love flows in abundance. Nevertheless, we need to challenge the notion that love is fickle and puny. Real love is not the stuff that we often see being called by love's name. In fact, maybe love has gotten a bad rap. Maybe too many of us have replaced the images that God intended to display love with our own definitions and ideas.

The Bible tells us that love is very patient and kind; yet we have known it to be impatient, easily annoyed, touchy, and arrogant. Paul says that love never fails; yet we see broken relationships, broken promises, and failed fellowship opportunities all around us in our families, our churches, and our communities. Yes, the Bible declares that now abides faith, hope, and love, these three and the greatest of these is love. However, it does not tell us that the greatness of love hinges on our ability to hope against all odds and to have faith in the most impossible of situations.

This week we will study love for the express purpose of reinvigorating our hearts and minds about it. Our challenge is to refocus ourselves on the true definition of love, as displayed by God, and then to spread that real love every place that we go. All this love is available because the Source of love (God) never runs out, and if we stay rightly connected to Love incarnate—Jesus—neither will we.

Questions to consider: Do you look for love in hidden or difficult places? Have you ever tried to pass something that you know is less than real love off as love? What is the hardest thing for you about displaying love to others? What is the easiest or best thing to you about sharing love with others? How do you receive and respond to love from others?

Day 2–Let's Go a Little Deeper

This is how everyone will recognize that you are my disciples—when they see the love you have for each other. (John 13:35 MSG)

The most controversial and confusing thing about love is not so much *what* it is or knowing *when* it is present. But rather, the distressing thing about love for most of us is *how* it acts. If you love someone or someone loves you, how are you supposed to interact with them? Falling in love, we can all do that, but how do we stay in love? Loving when times are easy and the recipient is lovable is a joy. How to keep on loving when we have been rebuffed or mistreated; **this** is the question to which an answer can seem so elusive.

Once on an episode of the hit ABC series *Scandal*, Edison said to Olivia, "Love isn't supposed to hurt . . ." And, while this line was stunning and profound, it is not necessarily true. Sometimes we hurt those whom we love. And yet, more important than the hurt is the fact that true, authentic love overcomes and fights through painful experiences.

So, the only real way to answer the question about how love acts is to look at the One who created love in the first place. God is love and God is the one true Source of love. If we want to have loving relationships, we must allow the Holy Spirit to transform our heart and mind. For only then, will we be able to love like God loves. 1 John 4 says it this way:

> Dear Friends, let us love one another, for love comes from God. Everyone who loves has been *born* of God and *knows* God. Whoever does not love does not know God, because God is love. (7–8 NIV, emphasis added)

Thus, the picture of perfect love for humanity is not found on the television or movie screen. Perfect love is this, "For God so loved the world that He gave His only begotten Son, that whosoever believes in Him should not perish but have everlasting life." (John 3:16 NKJV)

When God wanted to show love, God expressed love in an active, tangible, and meaningful way. God gave. And this is our challenge and our joyful delight, as we traverse through life: to live a life that continuously gives and shows the love of God to the world.

We love God because God first loved us. (See 1 John 4:19) We give God's love away to one another because God has poured perfect love into our hearts for that very purpose. (See Romans 5:5) Love is one thing that we must keep in the forefront of our minds. We must ensure that not a day or a season goes by in which we do not deliberately and meaningfully express love to God, to ourselves, and to others. In fact, one way that we can look at improving the quality and quantity of love expressed through our lives is by establishing a pattern or practice of being loving.

So, today, consider how you can give true expression to the love of God that is within you. It starts by simply being thankful to God for loving you with agape love—love that is unconditional, sacrificial, and redeeming. The next step is to express the love of God to everyone you meet each day. We do not necessarily express love to everyone in the same way, or to the same degree; but nevertheless, we practice showing love. Admittedly, this is not always easy. We can do it only by the power of Jesus Christ working within us. Through Christ we can do all things. (See Philippians 4:13) God has given us various ways of expressing love to God and to one another. Ways such as:

a. Spending quality time
b. Verbally expressing our love (out loud!)
c. Physically expressing love—there is great power in a touch, and unfortunately many people do not experience even a simple hug on a regular basis
d. Giving cards, gifts, and tokens to remind others of our love
e. Responding in positive ways to the opinions and affirmations of those whom we love

Let us not selfishly keep all this love that God has given us to ourselves. Let us practice giving love away. Remembering that, "Love doesn't make the world go round; love is what makes the ride worthwhile." (Franklin P. Jones)

Day 3–Learning from Our Experiences

Recall and reflect or journal about a time when you felt the sincere love of God. Think also about what ways you typically display love; first—to yourself, and second—to those closest to you. Are there new ways that you can incorporate into your pattern?

Meditate upon the following verses. Consider how you can focus more intently on loving God with all these aspects of yourself; your heart, your soul, your mind, and your strength. What would it look like for you to love more? More importantly, what would it look like if you loved better?

Mark 12:28b-31: Which command is the most important of all? This is the most important, Jesus answered: Listen, Israel! The Lord our God, the Lord is One. Love the Lord your God with all your heart, with all your soul, with all your mind, and with all your strength. The second is: Love your neighbor as yourself. There is no other command greater than these. (NIV)

Day 4–Biblical Character Reflection: Hosea

The Old Testament book of Hosea tells a complicated story to say the least. Nevertheless, the heart of the matter is love. In fact, the Life Application Study Bible describes the book this way: "The Book of Hosea is a love story—real, tragic and true." (Introduction to Hosea, pg. 1628) The main characters in the book are the prophet Hosea, Gomer (his wayward wife), and their children—some of which are fathered by men other than Hosea. Yet, the real story told through the book of Hosea is about how much God loves God's chosen people. God is committed to the children of Israel and that commitment never waivers. They (we) stray away, but God never abandons. They (we) disobey, but God remains faithful. They (we) follow the desire of their own hearts, but God beckons, entices, pursues, and draws them (us) back home again and again.

We see throughout this story the very principles which we have discussed and studied over the last three days. The fact is that the Israelites must endure the consequences and repercussions of their waywardness, backsliding, and disobedience. Nevertheless, God affirms, confirms, and affirms again that God's love is still available, accessible, and true. That's Love!

Take the time to read or listen to the fourteen chapters of the book of Hosea. You will be amazed. As you listen, let your mind, heart, and spirit absorb the truth that God loves you just as much as the children of Israel. God's commitment to you is no different today than it was to them all those many years ago. What love God has for you! What love God has for the world that God wants to bring through you, just as God loved Gomer through Hosea. What an amazing love!

Days 5-7—Making the Connection. Moving Forward.

This week we have focused upon the truth that there is an abundance of love available to us from God. The reality is that this love is not just for us, but also God intends for real love to flow in and through our lives to others. God uses us as conduits so that love can get to the utmost ends of the earth and world. For our lives to be a vehicle through which God's love flows freely, we must pay attention to what we believe about love. Moreover, we must be deliberate about how we live love out each day to everyone with whom we come in contact.

Before we leave our study on love, consider these characteristics about how love behaves. We can use these as markers or tests to see if what we are saying and doing as love really is love. Remember, we can call anything love, but in the end, only that which endures, sustains, encourages, blesses, and ultimately leads to salvation counts as God's true love. Here is what you must remember about the love of God as seen through Jesus Christ:

Christ's Love Is Forgiving. This is perhaps the most critical characteristic about Christ's love, and yet we have a hard time being convinced of its truth. Listen, no matter what you have done, or how many times you have done it; no matter what you allow, or how many promises you may break on your way to wholeness; God still loves you.

God's love is not wishy-washy. Understand, God will not let you get away with everything or live any kind of way for the sake of love. No, the love of God requires that you be accountable, responsible, and getting progressively better. Yet and still, when you stumble along the way, God is always ready and willing to forgive you. (See 1 John 1:9)

Many of us have found ourselves in the position of having sinned, and our sin has been due to our own pride, our own selfishness, our own bad judgment, and poor choices. We try and we fail. Well, the good news for us is that despite our sins, failures, and shortcomings, Christ forgives. Christ still wants to maintain the relationship and all we must do is come and acknowledge our wrong and accept Christ's offer of reconciliation. Unlike in the world where people hold your mistakes over your head, waiting and even seeking for an opportunity to remind you of your failures, Christ's love says, your failures do not disqualify you from relationship and service. When we know this for ourselves, then we can truly allow God to express this kind of love through us to the world. Christ's love is forgiving.

Yet the proof of God's amazing love is this: that it was while we were sinners that Christ died for us. (Romans 5:8 Phillips NT)

Christ's Love Is Empowering. Christ's love does not drain us, exhaust us, and wear us down. Instead, the love that God has for us inspires, motivates, and empowers us to be better and do better each day. Understand this: God does not command or call us to do something without also empowering us to carry it out. This is true even when it comes to helping us love according to God's standard.

When you know that God intends to use you not necessarily because of your ability, but more so because of your availability, then you can lean into the empowering love of Christ. Stop hesitating about doing what Christ is commanding or calling you to do because you do not see how it's possible. God can handle your feelings of inadequacy and God has already accounted for your stumbles and delays. God loves you enough to prod, push, and empower you toward your destiny.

Jesus replied, "All who love me will do what I say. My Father will love them, and we will come and make our home with each of them." (John 14:23 NLT)

Christ's Love Is Affirming. To say that Christ's love affirms means that it comes close at those times when others would pull their love away. Love is quite possibly the strongest force known to humanity. And when we know that we are affirmed, for who we are and for what we do, there is literally no limit to how far we can go. This is what Christ does. Even when we make mistakes, Christ does not withdraw from us. Christ does not cast us aside when we prove that we have some learning and growing to do. No, instead Christ comes to where we are and says from right where you are, draw close to me, follow me, and serve me. Christ does this because He knows that as we fall more in love with Jesus each day, we will grow; we will mature; and we will serve God in new, different, and better ways. Be grateful that Christ meets you at the point of every failure, every deficiency, and every weakness and says His love will sustain you, mature you, and grow you to the ultimate place that He has for you. That's affirmation!

Let us endeavor to live each day displaying the kind of love that God can truly use to transform and redeem the world. There are so many people all around us each day who need real, authentic, and compassionate love. It was because of this type of love that God sent Jesus to save the world once and for all. Now, God wants to make the world better and better by partnering with us who trust in Jesus to spread all this love around. So, come on, let God use you!

I love those who love me, and those who seek me find me. (Proverbs 8:17 NIV)

Week 6–Perseverance

Dealing with Delays, Disappointments, and Denials

Week 6–Perseverance
Dealing with Delays, Disappointments, and Denials

"Delayed answers to prayer are not only trials of faith; they also give us opportunities to honor God through our steadfast confidence in [God] even when facing the apparent denial of our request."

(Charles H. Spurgeon)

The greatest goal of our prayers should never be simply the outright answers. The highest aim of our prayer life should be intimacy and communion with the Lord. Whether we get what we want, we can have a closer, more committed relationship with God when we pray. Moreover, we can gain deeper understanding about who God is as we watch how God works. There is much to be discerned about God beyond simply **when** God will move. The beauty of a growing relationship is the ability to move from the surface question of *when* and get to know the *why* and *how* of God's methods. We will never know it all. Nevertheless, the best way to deal with delays, disappointments, and denials is to watch God, not our clocks. Sincere, vulnerable, faith-filled communion with God will not and cannot disappoint us if we keep our hearts fixed upon the Gift Giver and not merely upon the gifts.

It is very true what James says, "Every good gift and every perfect gift is from above, and comes down from the Father of lights, with whom there is no variation or shadow of turning." (James 1:17 NKJV) The times when God allows us to wait, when we have to truly persevere in our faith, are the times when we can come to trust the character of God. In the Message Bible, James 1:17c reads like this: ". . . There is nothing deceitful in God, nothing two-faced, nothing fickle." James tells us what God is *not*, to convince us about the essential attributes of God. It is usually difficult, if not impossible, to prove a negative; but in the case of Yahweh, it can be done by observation, attentiveness, and experience. When we develop a dynamic relationship with God, we will learn who God is. The problem is that as life unfolds with its delays, disappointments, and denials, we can become distracted from watching God; and instead, pay more attention to our circumstances.

What James writes is true, but all too often in life it is challenging to trust God's reputation. The fact of the matter is that the best way we can learn that God is true to form, (that God is not a liar and that God is reliable) is not by reading about God in a book, but by experiencing God through a personal relationship with Jesus Christ. In other words, we must faithfully, patiently, and courageously deal with our delays, disappointments, and denials because on the other side of the trial is the God who can be trusted. (See Psalm 9:10)

This week we will look at the attributes of God with the aim of developing and deepening our ability to persevere and trust. Trust must be practiced. Habits are formed by repetition. Thus, as we repeatedly practice trusting God—believing who God is and what God says—our faith will grow and our quality of life will improve.

The righteous cry out, and the Lord hears them; he delivers them from all their troubles. The Lord is close to the brokenhearted and saves those who are crushed in spirit. The righteous person may have many troubles, but the Lord delivers him from them all; he protects all his bones, not one of them will be broken. (Psalm 34:17–20 NIV)

Questions to consider: In what area(s) do you find it hard to trust God? Recall a time when you deliberately relied upon Christ to come through in a certain circumstance. What was the outcome? How did it feel to persevere?

Day 2–Let's Go a Little Deeper

For God is not unjust. He will not forget how hard you have worked for Him and how you have shown your love to Him by caring for other believers, as you still do. (Hebrews 6:10 NLT)

Several years ago, a gospel music artist by the name of Tonex released a song entitled "God Has Not 4got." The song simply affirms that if God said it, no matter how long ago it was, God still intends to do it. God has not forgotten; and indeed, when it comes to fulfilling God's Word, God does not forget. One reason why the song is so powerful is because it speaks of the character and faithfulness of God. The same God who loved humanity and remembered us when we were lost in sin and sent Jesus Christ to be our Savior, is the same God who still keeps promises.

The first life situation we are seeking to better handle this week is **delays**. *Rightly dealing with our delays helps us to gain a better understanding of the faithfulness of God.* God does not forget. So, if there is a delay, there must be a *God* reason for it. A God reason is always a good reason. Ultimately, delays are for our protection and benefit, to keep us from mishandling a blessing or squandering an opportunity. Sometimes delays are a consequence of our sinful behavior or erroneous choices.

Consider the children of Israel. An entire generation was required to wander in the wilderness because they did not trust God's word and God's character. Essentially, it happened like this. God said, "I have given you this land (Canaan), go and possess it." They said, "The inhabitants are too big, too strong, and too numerous. We cannot see how to defeat them. We will not do it." In other words, they did not trust God to do what God said. (See Numbers 13 and 14) Therefore, the generation that doubted God forfeited its chance to enter the Promised Land and the next generation had to wait forty years for their ancestors to die before it could move forward.

Sometimes delays are not about us at all, but rather about the plan that God has ordained for our lives. In such cases, delays are not really delays per se. It is that God's timing is different from ours. God has a set time, an exact moment, when circumstances and people will line up in our favor. Certain doors simply will not open until God says that it is time, no matter how long or how hard we may stand there knocking.

Ultimately, no matter what the reason is for the delay, the point is that we must handle it with faith. We learn to hope and persevere when we wait. After we wait and God comes through, we know in a way that we never did before that God will take care of us and that we can handle much more in life than we ever thought we could. Our waiting is made easier when we remember God can be trusted, no matter how long things take.

Disappointments are a little different than delays. On one level, being disappointed hurts more than simply being delayed because disappointment means that your expected outcome is not merely "late," but will never be achieved. When we are disappointed, it is critical to be honest with ourselves, with the other person (if applicable), and with God. You see, *we best handle disappointments by submitting to God's wisdom.* Things did not work out as you had hoped or expected. Now what? Trust God and reaffirm your willingness to submit to God's best for your life. It is hard to reconcile that God's best could be anything different than our desired outcome. Nevertheless, these are the times when we must yield to God's knowledge, which is greater; God's vision, which goes further; and God's ways, which are always better than ours.

Viewed properly (faithfully), disappointments are an opportunity to envision another outcome. Sometimes what we want simply is not what God wants. When our plans get interrupted or disturbed, we have a chance to refocus on God and watch God's perfect plan unfold. When we are disappointed, we should refocus our energy away from our feelings and toward our decision to keep working and to keep moving.

Denials are an altogether different scenario than delays and disappointments. At first thought you may think that disappointments and denials are the same; however, they are not. Denials are those times when we absolutely get refused. God says no and it is definitive. A disappointment may be that we applied for a job and did not get it, but we eventually get a different job. A denial, on the other hand, is when we pray for our loved one to be healed, and yet the healing we wanted never comes.

Denials are tough. Nevertheless, there are valuable lessons to be learned when we handle even our denials with honesty and faith. *Denials can teach us about God's sovereignty.* Denials help to cultivate peace deep down in our hearts because we learn to know God separately from what God gives. You see faithful obedience and trust that is the result of getting what we want, or something even better, is not God's ultimate goal for our life. God wants us to be malleable, to be trusting, and to be willing to go along with whatever choice God makes because we understand that we belong to God. And we understand that God does not make mistakes. This does not mean that we are not allowed to be sad, to grieve, and to mourn our denials, however they might come. It just means that even during our range of emotions, we trust in God and in God's sovereign will for us.

It is like what the prophet Jeremiah learned when God showed him how the potter deals with the clay in Jeremiah 18. Jeremiah writes: "Family of Israel, can't I do the same thing with you?" says the LORD. "You are in my hands like the clay in the potter's hands." (Verse 6 NCV) As Christians, we are in God's hands. God can shape us, reshape us, mold us, remold us; God can and will do whatever God pleases. Nevertheless, as we study God's character we will come to learn that whatever God allows, whatever God brings, or does not bring, can be made to work together for our ultimate good. It can help us become more like Jesus. The beautiful thing about God's sovereignty is that it gives us reason to always have hope. God is never defeated, intimidated, or undone. God always has a perfect plan and God always has the wisdom, courage, power, and strength to bring that plan to pass. God. Can. Be. Trusted.

Any discussion about denials and God's sovereignty is incomplete, however, if we do not also consider the fact that evil is a reality of the fallen state of humanity and our world. We must guard against adopting a mind-set that makes God responsible for the works of the enemy. It is very hard to reconcile that "bad" things happen to "good" people. It is a conundrum, of sorts, to realize that God does not stop every unpleasant thing that goes on in our world.

However, the reality is that God made humans with a free will. It would be outside of God's nature for God to snatch that free will back from us. We cannot get off the hook for our own behaviors, be they systemic and individual, by "blaming" God. Evil exists, and this is why we need to be in a growing, dynamic relationship with God, by knowing Jesus Christ. We can pray for peace, for protection, for provision, and we must also work for these things. We can do our best to make sure that we do not allow our lives to be used as instruments of the enemy. The way we do this is by staying as connected to Christ as possible, being willing to allow God to mold us into the image of Jesus Christ daily. In the end, whether it is a delay, a disappointment, or a denial, we must remember that God is credible and trustworthy and has a good plan for our lives.

Even youths grow tired and weary, and young men stumble and fall; but those who hope in the Lord will renew their strength. They will soar on wings like eagles; they will run and not grow weary, they will walk and not be faint. (Isaiah 40:30–31 NIV)

Day 3–Learning from Our Experiences

Recall and reflect or journal about a time when you experienced a delay, a disappointment, or a denial. Feel free to think about more than one. What did you learn about God's character through these experiences? Considering our discussion about these three concepts, re-evaluate your experiences. Seek to gain a fresh understanding about God's faithfulness, wisdom, and sovereignty.

Meditate upon the following verses:

Jeremiah 18:1–6: This is the word the LORD spoke to Jeremiah: "Go down to the potter's house, and I will give you my message there." So, I went down to the potter's house and saw him working at the potter's wheel. He was using his hands to make a pot from clay, but something went wrong with it. So, he used that clay to make another pot the way he wanted it to be. Then the LORD spoke his word to me: "Family of Israel, can't I do the same thing with you?" says the LORD. "You are in my hands like the clay in the potter's hands." (NCV)

Do you believe that God has good plans for your life? When you are honest with yourself, do you focus more upon your plans for yourself or God's plans for you? You can learn the answer to this question by considering how you handle your delays, disappointments, and denials. How can you stay more focused upon the character and nature of God each day?

Day 4–Biblical Character Reflection: Paul

Paul, a former persecutor of the Christian Church, wrote most of the books and letters that comprise the New Testament. His journey, from non-believer to convert to prophet to the Gentiles (non-Jewish), was quite eventful. No matter where we are along our faith journey, Paul can be an example to us.

A significant part of his journey is detailed in the book the Acts of the Apostles. Through it all, Paul experienced quite a few delays, disappointments, and denials. His life affirms that those who will be used mightily by God must be flexible, humble, and strong enough to deal with all three. Paul's journey is filled with too many ups, downs, and in-betweens to count, but nevertheless let's consider Acts 16:6–7 as an example of the many things that Paul endured.

Paul and his companions traveled throughout the region of Phrygia and Galatia, *having been kept by the Holy Spirit from preaching the word* in the province of Asia. When they came to the border of Mysia, they tried to enter Bithynia, *but the Spirit of Jesus would not allow them to.* (NIV, emphasis added)

At first glance it is strange that Paul and his companions would be prevented, even forbidden, from preaching the gospel of Jesus Christ. Yet, Luke tells us that at least these two times, Paul had a plan and he was faced with a denial. This suggests to us a couple of important truths. When we are faced with a delay, disappointment, and/or denial, we must remember these truths. We too can have an experience like Paul and his companions, if instead of pushing against God when we are presented with a delay, denial, or disappointment, we continue to trust and seek God to unfold God's desired plan. That is what happened in Acts 16:8–10. God refused to let them go one way, because God was preparing to lead them in another direction.

Here are two truths to remember:

God has a plan. This is what we focused on in yesterday's passage. We must continually (daily and even multiple times a day) remind ourselves that God is deliberate, intentional, and careful about the lives of those who have put their faith in Jesus Christ. No matter how it looks or feels in the natural, God's plan is unfolding and will come to pass. God forbid that we miss it because our eyes linger too long on the troubles of life instead of upon the Sustainer of it.

God has a promise. Again, this is not a new point. We should be continuously in the word of God, seeking out the truths and promises of God. Start a promise journal. Make a list of all your prayer requests, and then put alongside them the promise to which that desire corresponds. If you cannot find a promise for it, take the time to consider if the desire is truly from God. If you have a promise, keep reciting and remembering that truth, until it is within your grasp.

Days 5-7–Making the Connection. Moving Forward.

This week, we have established that the best way to deal with delays, disappointments, and denials is to focus on the character of God. God has much to show you about who God is when you are required to wait, persevere, and even to simply let go of your desired outcomes. We will begin to live our best life once we learn to believe that no matter what we are going through, God is; God is faithful; and God can be trusted.

In fact, most of the times when we find ourselves in situations that require us to hold out, to wait, and to press into our faith, are times when Jesus wants to mature us and take us to new levels in God. It may not always be clear on the surface what God is doing, which is why we must be convinced about the character and reputation of God. Despite how we feel and what we see, "Let us hold unswervingly to the hope we profess, for he who promised is faithful." (Hebrews 10:23 NIV)

As we close out this topic, let's go back to a text that was referenced earlier in the week. Hebrews 6:10 says, "God is not unjust; he will not forget your work and the love you have shown him as you have helped his people and continue to help them." (NIV) This verse reminds us that God can be trusted. The writer of Hebrews says it plainly; God is not unjust. God will not forget your hard work, or the love and faithfulness you have shown to God's people. When you are experiencing delays, disappointments, and denials—keep your eyes on God. Rehearse the reasons why you trust God. Repeat over and over again the truth that you know about God's character. Review God's reputation. Do not let the fact that things are not happening as fast as or in the way that you want them to, to cause you to lose hope. Yet hope in God! Trust God's timing and trust God's plan. God's plan is much better than you could ever imagine. Keep the faith.

Spend time over the next couple of days coming up with an affirmation of at least ten scriptural truths, which you want to see manifested in and through your life. Recite this affirmation at least once a week, daily if possible. Do this and watch your faith begin to grow. Remember, ". . . faith comes from hearing, that is, hearing the Good News about Christ." (Romans 10:17 NLT) When you repeatedly hear and confess the truth about Christ, faith is built up. Your faith cannot grow unless and until you make learning and reciting the word of God a priority. Start today. It will be well worth the investment of your time.

Week 7–Faith

Do You Believe This?

Week 7–Faith
Do You Believe This?

Jesus said to her, "I am the resurrection and the life. Those who believe in me, even though they die, will live, and everyone who lives and believes in me will never die. Do you believe this?" She said to him, "Yes, Lord, I believe that you are the Messiah, the Son of God, the one coming into the world." (John 11:25–27 NRSV)

So much about life and how we handle it depends upon the answer to this simple question: Do you believe that Jesus is who He says He is? It may seem overly simplistic. It may even seem like a super-spiritual question. But, it is not. The truth is, no matter what happens in your life—who comes, who goes, what triumph or tragedy you endure—your ability to overcome depends upon the power of God operating in and through you. The way we access God's power is through our faith and belief in Jesus Christ. (See 1 John 5:4–5)

One thing which can make believing difficult is the fact that we misunderstand the nature of it. Often, we understand belief to be something that happens one time. So, when we think about being in the family of God, we quote what the apostle Paul said in Romans 10:9, "If you declare with your mouth, 'Jesus is Lord,' and believe in your heart that God raised Him from the dead, you will be saved." (NIV) This is certainly true. Nevertheless, to truly grab hold to what this verse is saying, we must know that believing is not a single incidence. Belief is something that happens repeatedly. We establish a pattern of belief in our lives and that belief allows us to see more and more of God over time.

So, we entrust ourselves to Christ, for protection, for salvation, for peace and guidance, for life, but we do so moment by moment. We believe yes, and we keep on believing throughout the course of our lives. This is an important concept to grasp because life often attacks us at the level of our belief. Jesus knew this and that is why when He was on earth He performed miracles and presented Himself to His disciples for the express purpose of helping them to believe. The same is true today. Even though Jesus is no longer physically present on earth, He is yet living and revealing Himself to be God day by day. We must have eyes of faith to see Him and hearts of obedience to follow where and how Jesus leads.

Our goal this week is twofold: 1) to help us to see that Christ is living and moving all around us each day, and 2) to give us tools that will help us to continuously replenish our belief in Christ daily.

Questions to consider: Have you ever asked God to show you who God is? Are you open to seeing and learning new things about God each day? Recall a time when your eyes were open and you believe you saw God moving in or around your life. What makes you doubt God?

Day 2–Let's Go a Little Deeper

Then Jesus said to the disciples, "Have faith in God. I tell you the truth, you can say to this mountain, 'May you be lifted up and thrown into the sea,' and it will happen. But you must really believe it will happen and have no doubt in your heart." (Mark 11:22, 23 NLT)

There is a critical aspect about belief, which we sometimes overlook. That is that belief not only includes faith, but it also includes a decision not to doubt. The days and times in which we live are full of reasons to be doubtful. We are living in a *verify-everything culture.* Hollywood and the media drive our incessant need to uncover, debunk, and substantiate everyone and nearly everything. Google puts this power at our fingertips. Wikipedia has made us all experts. Yet, all this information and investigating does not necessarily serve to make us more knowledgeable; but rather, it give cause and reason to be filled with doubt.

We doubt ourselves; we doubt those around us; we doubt our circumstances; and if we are not careful, we will let all this doubting spread into our thinking about God and God's Word. God does not need to be authenticated. God is, whether we believe or not. We would do well to banish our doubting and learn to trust. The thing about doubt is that it is a cancer to belief and it undermines faith. If we are going to continuously see and believe God, we must get a handle on our doubt. We must be sure to have tools and practices in place to guard our hearts, our minds, and our spirits. Because when it comes to the presence, power, and principles of Jesus Christ operating in our lives, there is no room for doubt. We must be alert and vigilant because, like cancer, doubt can invade and spread destructively and oftentimes undetected.

One of the questions to ponder from yesterday's lesson was, "What makes you doubt God?" This is an important question because many times we doubt God and do not realize it. Or, what is more likely the case, we allow our unreasonable, unfounded doubts to linger and go unchecked in our minds. We have all had life experiences which should convince us that Jesus Christ can be trusted. Nevertheless, in the midst of the storm, doubt will creep in and cause us to take our eyes off God and focus on the person or predicament that is troubling us. The encouragement for us today is the same admonishment that Jesus gave to his disciple Thomas in John 20:27, "Do not doubt, but believe!"

As you read Thomas' story today in John 20:24–29, think about how you can guard against doubt in your life. Remember, it is not enough to simply believe; you must remove the doubt. Doubting is a choice. Belief is its antidote.

Day 3–Learning from Our Experiences

Recall and reflect or journal about a time when you doubted God. What was it about the situation that caused you to doubt that

God was willing and able to move on your behalf? How did you combat your doubt?

Meditate upon the following verses and consider whether you find it easier to believe God or to doubt God. Talk to Jesus about your areas of unbelief. Ask God to help you to believe.

Mark 9:21–24: How long has this been happening to him? Jesus asked his father. "From childhood," he said. "And many times, it has thrown him into fire or water to destroy him. But if You can do anything, have compassion on us and help us." Then Jesus said to him, **"If You can? Everything is possible to the one who believes." Immediately the father of the boy cried out, "I do believe! Help my unbelief."** (HCSB, emphasis added)

Day 4–Biblical Character Reflection: Thomas

We read Thomas' story two days ago in John 20:24–29. Thomas shows us that doubt is a real possibility, even for those who walk very closely with Jesus. Faith does not exempt you from having doubts; faith helps you to keep doubt in the proper perspective. It is not a bad thing to have doubt; we all go through times when our faith is tested. The bad thing is to let doubt pervade our thinking so much that we start to believe it over the truth.

The truth is that God, more than anyone else in our lives, has proven to be worthy of our trust and faithful to every word God has ever spoken. Yet and still, even with that perfect track record, we are prone to be fainthearted, fearful, and forgetful every day. We must be honest about our doubts with God because we can only fight the battle that we recognize. If we do not admit that doubt is present, or a possibility, it will be very difficult for us to guard against it. In fact, more of us should be like Thomas.

Despite having doubt, here are a few things that Thomas did, which we can also do. First, he was honest. He admitted that he had doubt and was not willing to believe to his trusted friends, those who knew him and who knew Jesus. Second, he stayed in the fellowship. Yes, Thomas was absent when Jesus came the first time, but he did not abandon the fellowship; he stayed in position and kept coming to the places where Jesus had been and where he could be influenced by other believers. Third, he stayed open to seeing and receiving something new from Jesus. Even though Thomas did not believe, he was still open to believing in the future. It is unfortunate that he put conditions on his belief; nevertheless, at least he was willing to receive fresh revelation and better understanding about Jesus in his life. He did not believe, but he still had a desire to see and to touch Jesus.

If we can do the things that Thomas did, we will find that Jesus will respond to us in similar ways. When we are open, honest, sincere, and still looking to see Jesus, even from our place of doubt, Jesus will come to us. Jesus will give us what we need. Jesus will help our unbelief.

Days 5-7–Making the Connection. Moving Forward.

This week we have been wrestling with the principle of belief. We have learned that belief includes not only our faith, but also our decision to not doubt. We understand that our ability to have and maintain our belief in Christ, despite the times and the seasons of life, opens us up to unlimited possibilities. In fact, when we have unwavering belief in God, nothing shall be impossible for us. When we believe in the power, authority, presence, and truth of Jesus Christ, there is no closed door, which God cannot open. There is no mountain over which God will not help us to climb.

We have also seen that Jesus loves us enough to come to us, care for us, and carry us out of our areas of unbelief. The truth is that when we are struggling with doubt, only God really knows how to help us. We may regain our strength and faith through a song, a sermon, a word of testimony, or just from a passing conversation with a stranger. The key is that we must stay connected to God and to other believers. We, like Thomas, must have a community of believers with whom we can be brutally honest. We need to develop some authentic friendships where we can admit that we doubt the

...oubtable God. Remember, to doubt every now and then is not bad. But, allowing doubt to persist in your mind, heart, and spirit can be deadly. Do not doubt; believe!

As we leave this topic, be encouraged by knowing that you can develop tools and strategies to combat doubt in your life. You do not have to let doubt and fear rule your life. You do not have to be fragile and fainthearted every time contrary winds blow. Here are some ways that you can build your belief in the power, authority, and person of Jesus Christ as you journey.

Persist in God's Presence. Do not allow anyone or anything to keep you away from God, not even your doubt. When your faith is being tested is the time when you must persist—linger, abide, and remain—in the presence of God. Increase your times of study, prayer, and meditation during the hard times. Do not let your thoughts drive you away from Christ; take every thought captive and make it obey the truth of God's Word. (See 2 Corinthians 10:5)

Practice Your Profession of Faith. Keep repeating what you know and what you believe about God. When doubts come, remind yourself about what you already know and what you have already experienced with Christ. We know that our profession of faith is critical because the Bible says that ". . . it is with your mouth that you profess your faith and are saved." (Romans 10:10b NIV) We can increase our belief simply by repetition and redundancy. Put your faithful expressions of hope in God on repeat. Say what you believe, and eventually you will see and experience what you said.

Predict the Promises. The next time you are struggling with doubt and having a hard time believing that Jesus will come through, take the time to predict which promise of God applies to your situation. Use your *CSI*-like investigative skills to find promises in God's Word. Then, make a prediction about the way that God will come through based upon what you have heard, read, and seen God do in the past. Remain open to allowing God to do what is best (God always does what is best), but nevertheless, you can fortify yourself by guessing exactly which promise God will fulfill through your current predicament. Your faith will increase as you keep standing on the promises of God.

Jesus performed many other signs in the presence of His disciples that are not written in this book. But these are written so that you may believe Jesus is the Messiah, the Son of God, and by believing you may have life in His name. (John 20:30–31 HCSB)

Week 8–Grace
The Goodness of Grace

Week 8–Grace
The Goodness of Grace

. . . The grace of Christ is the only good ground for life . . .
(Hebrews 13:9 MSG)

Grace is often defined as God's unmerited favor or receiving what we do not deserve. This is true and it is also much more than that. Grace is the energy and power by which we are saved. It is the way that our lives are transformed for Jesus Christ. Grace is the way that God gets our attention and it is the means through which we stay connected to God, through Jesus Christ. There is never a time or an instance, whether you are saved or still in the process of making that decision, when grace is not at work in and around your life. Grace is the active agent, which allows you to do, to be, and to become all that God dreams for you. Moreover, it is the sustaining strength, peace, and wisdom that enables you to endure the rigorous process of doing, being, and becoming.

As powerful and good as grace is, many of us are negligent in recognizing and giving God credit for it on a consistent basis. Because grace is all around us all the time, it can often be overlooked in the same way that we pass by the beauty of flowers and trees and barely notice them. The fact of the matter is grace is too important, necessary, and effective for us not to see it and give thanks to God for it each and every day. Therefore, we must shift our perspective about grace so that we can understand that not only are we recipients of it, but also, we are to be conduits of grace to others. God infuses our lives with grace so that we can be able to carry grace everywhere that we go.

This week we will focus on getting to know what grace is and improving our ability to see its beauty and work in our lives; for grace, truly is good.

For it is by grace you have been saved, through faith—and this is not from yourselves, it is the gift of God—not by works, so that no one can boast. (Ephesians 2:8–9 NIV)

Questions to consider: What is your personal definition of grace? What does grace look like to you? Keep a grace log for the next seven days in which you capture thoughts about your interactions with the grace that is all around you.

Day 2—Let's Go a Little Deeper

From His fullness we have all received, grace upon grace. (John 1:16 NRSV)

One of the first and most important truths we must know about grace is that we have all received it, in abundance. To grasp this truth, we need to expand our understanding of what grace is. As mentioned yesterday, the typical definition that we hear of grace is "God's unmerited favor." And, while this is certainly true, this is a rather one-dimensional view of grace. However, grace is multidimensional. One of the best descriptions of grace is given by Maurice Bassali in his book entitled, *Praise: The Door to God's Presence.* Bassali says:

> A three-fold divine ministry and undertaking in grace is described in the New Testament. First, God *saves* sinners by grace (Eph. 2:8). Second, God *keeps* through grace those who are saved; they are said to "stand" in grace (Rom 5:2; 1 Pet. 5:12). Third, God teaches in grace those who are saved and kept as to how they should live to God's eternal glory (Titus 2:12). (P. 58, emphasis in original)

So, we can see that grace is complex and can look very different depending upon our situation or circumstance. In fact, grace can be understood as the broad category under which many other blessings and virtues of God fall. Grace can show up in our lives as comfort, peace, joy, strength, favor, and forgiveness; just to name a few. Grace can be an opened door in one instance and a closed door in another. Nevertheless, no matter how grace is manifested, it is always good and God always has a purpose and a plan for extending grace to us.

Our life experiences are designed to draw us closer to God and to align our character and thinking with that of Jesus Christ. God uses grace to draw us closer to God and then to transform us into the image of Christ. Grace is not merely about us being favored, preferred, and chosen by God. Grace is proof that we have not only been with God, but also that we have been changed through the experience of being with God. Some of us go through challenging, triumphant, electrifying, or distressing experiences and yet remain unchanged. The reason we do not change is because we merely seek to get through or get over our experiences instead of allowing the Holy Spirit to truly come into us—our thoughts, words, emotions, actions—and make us more like Christ in the process.

It takes grace to go through life and not become hardened. It takes grace to withstand the pressure to conform to the images that the world has set for you. It takes grace to be still and remain silent when there is so much you want to do and say. Being a recipient of God's grace means that you have been remade to look, think, and act like Christ.

In practice this means that we bless when cursing is justified. We extend compassion in the face of blatant attacks. We forgive even without being asked and we consider the needs of others more than we cater to our own. Moreover, growing in grace allows us to stand up again after failure. It gives us strength to admit when we have been wrong, helping us to apologize and move forward in humility. Grace not only helps us to recover from our falls, but also to be accountable to the right people, so that a fall can be prevented in the first place. It takes grace, grace, and more grace to live this life in a way that makes a real difference—for God and for those to whom you are connected.

When we understand the power and impact of grace, we will know that no failure, frailty, or fault—of our own or another—is greater than God. Renowned Christian writer Oswald Chambers once wrote, "We are not here to prove God answers prayer; we are here to be living monuments of God's grace." (*My Utmost for His Highest*, August 6) To be a monument of God's grace means that when people see and think of you, they will recall the goodness of Jesus Christ. God saves us by grace and sustains us through grace. God does this not only so we can know that being in relationship with God is beneficial, but also, so that we can convince or inspire others to trust God as well. A monument is an example of something. Our lives should be examples of God's truth, God's power, and God's grace. Live as a monument of God's grace today.

But to each one of us grace has been given as Christ apportioned it. (Ephesians 4:7 NIV)

Day 3–Learning from Our Experiences

Recall and reflect or journal upon a time when you recognized that you were a recipient of God's grace. How did that make you feel? What about a time when you were a conduit of grace? How did it make you feel to be an instrument of grace to another? What does it mean to you to grow in grace? Are you growing in grace?

Meditate upon the following verses and take time to thank God that you have been both a recipient and conduit of the good grace of God. Ask Jesus to show you how you can be a better steward of the manifold grace that you have received.

1 Peter 4:10: Like good stewards of the manifold grace of God, **serve** one another with whatever gift each of you has received. (NRSV, emphasis added)

2 Peter 3:18: Rather, you must **grow** in the grace and knowledge of our Lord and Savior Jesus Christ. All glory to him, both now and forever! Amen. (NLT, emphasis added)

Day 4–Biblical Character Reflection: Hagar

Read Hagar's story in Genesis chapters 16 and 21. She was the Egyptian maidservant of Sarai (later Sarah), who conceived and bore a child to Abram (later Abraham). At first glance we will determine that Hagar had a difficult journey and that life was unkind to her. And, while she certainly had some struggles and disappointments, Hagar was touched by God and she experienced God's grace.

Hagar conceived a son, Ishmael, who, while not the promised heir of Abraham, nevertheless became the father of many descendants. Hagar was forced to flee from mistreatment at the hands of Sarah and eventually she was banished from her family by the father of her son. Yet, Hagar was met by grace many times along her life's journey.

We see the goodness of grace in Hagar's life because when she fled from Sarah in Genesis chapter 16, the Lord sent an angel to meet her and give her comfort. The text says, "The angel of the LORD *found* Hagar near a spring in the desert . . ." (Genesis 16:7 NIV, emphasis added) Hagar was in a tough situation; she was running and had no real options, but God found her. Not only did the angel of the Lord find her, but also, he gave her comfort, instruction, and a promise. (See Genesis 16:9–10)

After Hagar's interaction with the angel of the Lord, she knows God in a new and different way. Genesis 16:13 says, "She gave this name to the LORD who spoke to her: 'You are the God who sees me,' for she said, 'I have now seen the One who sees me.'" (NIV) It was by God's grace that Hagar received the strength that she needed during a great time of conflict. We can learn from her story that even during our darkest moments of defeat and pain, by grace, God still finds us, speaks to us, and shows us which way to go. Whenever we can see or hear God, we know that we have experienced the goodness of grace. Moreover, even when God is seemingly silent and invisible, by God's grace, we can have the assurance that God still sees and hears us.

Later in Genesis 21, after giving birth to Ishmael, Hagar and the boy are sent away by Abraham. While thirsty and traveling through the desert, she fears for her life and the life of her young son. Again, God by grace hears and sees them and sends the provision that they need. From there, we are told that God was with Ishmael and he grew up and even married. When God's grace touches our lives, we can go further and do more than we ever dreamed or imagined. Hagar's life helps us to see this truth.

Days 5-7—Making the Connection. Moving Forward.

*But he said to me, "My grace is **sufficient** for you, for my power is **made perfect** in weakness." Therefore, I will boast all the more gladly about my weaknesses, so that **Christ's power** may rest on me. . . . For when I am weak, then I am strong.* (2 Corinthians 12:9–10b NIV, emphasis added)

This week we have gained new perspective and insight into the goodness of God's grace. After we understand what grace is and from where it comes, it is critical that we learn to truly appreciate its nature. As you are growing and learning to see grace in your own life, and extend grace to others, understand these truths about it.

Grace cannot be depleted. The Greek word for grace as used in 2 Corinthians 12:9 is *charis,* which literally means to be inexhaustible, never interrupted, and to know no bounds. God's grace is the source of all strength and life and, as such, it cannot be depleted or used up. Unlike our electronic devices which must continuously be charged, the grace of God is always on one hundred. Here is what the Bible says in 2 Corinthians 9:8 about the strength of grace: "And God *is* able to make **all grace abound** toward you, that you, always having **all sufficiency** in all *things*, may have an **abundance for every good work**." (NKJV, emphasis added) When we understand the nature of grace, we will see that we are never without hope or help. God makes sure that we are always able to do whatever is required by giving us God's power—through grace.

God chose to save us by grace (and not our works) for this very reason. If it was up to us, we would eventually quit and stop working. But, as it is, God's grace keeps saving us, sanctifying us, and strengthening us—not once, not twice, but over and over and over again. The grace of God can establish you and stabilize you in every situation, crisis, and dilemma of life. Just reach out with your faith and touch it because grace is always there in abundance.

Grace cannot be diluted. God's grace is not only always there, but also it is always powerful. It is good to have something in abundance, but what's more important is that it be powerful and effective. There are times in life when we are surrounded by a lot of people, but those individuals may not always have what we need. That is never the case with God or with the grace that God provides. God says the more grace that you need, the more grace you will have. Its power (God's power) will never be weakened; but rather, as we need more it becomes that much stronger.

In Romans, Paul describes the power of grace this way: "But where sin abounded, grace abounded **much more**." (5:20b NKJV, emphasis added) This suggests that there is a two-to-one correlation between our sin (need) and God's grace. When there is sin (or any need), there is not only grace, but more grace and in fact, much more grace available to us. God's ability to aid, empower, and strengthen us does not diminish when the task is more difficult. In fact, the opposite happens; it grows.

Moreover, grace is personal. God does not give us a one-size-fits-all dose of grace. God gives you the grace you need to fit each and every situation in your life. We do not need all the grace that exists, we simply need what is sufficient to meet the test. This is what God gives. And, since God knows exactly how much we need, God always gives us just the right amount of grace.

Grace can be discovered. No matter what the situation, circumstance, or need it is that we are facing, we can always find grace to help us. Grace can always be discovered. However, the way we discover it is by allowing ourselves to be weak and by expressing our needs to God and others. To truly discover grace in our lives, we must attain a perspective like Paul did in 2 Corinthians 12:10. We must learn to say that "for Christ's sake, I delight in weaknesses, in insults, in hardships, in persecutions, in difficulties. For when I am weak, then I am strong." (NIV) The key is that we do it for Christ's glory. Understand this: if God allows it, God certainly has a purpose and a plan for how to use it for our good and God's glory. God does not cause the evil, tragic, painful situations of our lives. Nevertheless, God can be found amid every circumstance and God can work everything together for our good. (See Romans 8:28)

We discover the grace of God, in God's presence, by coming boldly before God's throne. In Hebrews 4:16, we are encouraged to ". . . approach the throne of grace with boldness, so that we may receive mercy and **find grace** to help in time of need." (NRSV, emphasis added) We do not have to beg for it; we do not have to wish for it; all we must do is come to God with eyes of faith looking for it. When we come to Christ with open hearts, open hands, and hopeful minds, we can be sure that we will find the grace that we need. God hides grace in some of the most unusual, unexpected, and unlikely places. Therefore, we must stay connected to Christ to discover continuously all the grace that God has waiting for us. One of the best ways to see the goodness of God is to recognize the grace of God. When we experience God's goodness for ourselves, it will be our humble pleasure to pass it on to the world.

Grace and peace to you many times over as you deepen in your experience with God and Jesus, our Master. (2 Peter 1:2 MSG)

Week 9–Prayer
Let Us Pray

Week 9–Prayer
Let Us Pray

"Nothing lies beyond the reach of prayer except those things outside of the will of God."   (L. B. Cowman, *Streams in the Desert*, June 26)

Prayer is the most universal discipline of the Christian faith. Everything about believing in God is tied to an understanding that God hears us and responds to our prayers. And yet, prayer is also quite possibly the most universally misunderstood discipline of the Christian faith. We all do it (at least occasionally), but we are not always totally clear on what prayer is and how and why it is effective and powerful in our lives.

Theologian and Christian author Henri Nouwen once wrote that "prayer is a way of life." (*With Open Hands*, pg. 121) This is perhaps the one thing about prayer which we must continue to remember along our journey. We should not merely see prayer as an activity that we pause to do occasionally, periodically, or continuously; but rather, we should see prayer as our lifeline. We do not pray merely to get answers; we pray because prayer brings us into communion and communication with God. We do not pray to give God a laundry list of our desires. We pray because we believe that God loves us, is listening to us, and cares about the desires of our hearts. Prayer is one sure way for us to fulfill the instruction of Jesus given in John 15:4 to "Abide in Me . . ." (NKJV) Prayer is a consistent and deliberate means of abiding (remaining, dwelling, and living) in Christ. Each time that we bring our minds, hearts, and spirits to God in prayer, we are made better and stronger.

This week, we will dissect the principle of prayer with the hopes of expanding our understanding and appreciation for it, and more importantly, for the God with whom our prayer life is spent.

Jesus told them a story showing that it was necessary for them to pray consistently and never quit. (Luke 18:1 MSG)

Questions to consider: Can you honestly say that prayer is a consistent practice in your life? Why or why not? What questions do you have about prayer? Do you have a prayer closet or a place where you pray regularly? Do you have regular prayer partners?

Day 2–Let's Go a Little Deeper

O Lord, please hear my prayer! Listen to the prayers of those of us who delight in honoring you . . . (Nehemiah 1:11 NLT)

The starting point with any discussion is that we simplify and clarify our terms. Therefore, before we go any further, let's agree on our definition of prayer. What is it? We often think and hear that prayer is communicating with God, which usually means us telling God that we need (or want) something or someone to change in our lives. And, while an aspect of our time in prayer may certainly be spent talking to God, even about our wants and needs, that is not the purpose of prayer. More than simply communication with God, a better definition is the one used by Christian writer Claude King. King says that prayer is *"communion with* God." (*The Call to Follow Christ: Six Disciplines for New and Growing Believers*, pg. 46, emphasis added) Communion is more than talking; communing is connecting, sharing, intimacy, fellowship, accord, rapport, and conformity. So, prayer includes not merely talking but listening, silence, meditation, reading, writing, worship, praise, music, fasting, and partnership. When we expand our understanding about prayer, we can see how critical it is that we are continuously engaged in acts of prayer. Moreover, we can better understand how detrimental the lack of prayer is to our overall effectiveness in life.

Not only do we need to expand our definition of what prayer is, but also, we must widen our understanding of the purpose of prayer. In fact, one place where the mind of God and the minds of most of us diverge when it comes to prayer is in understanding its purpose. Prayer is its own reward. Prayer brings us into union and communion with the God of the universe. We need not wait for a *reason* to pray. Our primary reason to pray is always the same: because we have time, space, opportunity, and the desire to draw closer to God. So, the core of prayer is relationship; and the purpose of prayer is to create, maintain, and strengthen our relationship with God through our faith in Jesus Christ.

God is relational, and what happens in and around our lives is designed to help us to relate better to God. Prayer is one way that God provides us with an opportunity to know and understand who God is and how God operates. Prayer is a dynamic exchange. The more we give ourselves to prayer, the better we will be because we will know more about God. Moreover, by spending meaningful time with God, our lives will improve because we will become better able to recognize how and when God is working.

Like any other relationship, we get out of our relationship with God what we put into it. In fact, we receive much more through our relationship with God than we could ever put into it. But the point is, when we open our hearts and life up to Christ completely, Christ can open things up to us, in prayer, which we never dreamed of or imagined. God gives us wisdom, power, and authority through having an active and disciplined prayer life. Being engaged in prayer is its own reward and it is beneficial to us, even if we never receive any of our petitions, which is unlikely.

Our best model for an effective prayer life is Jesus. Jesus always took time to get alone with God and pray. Jesus, being fully God and fully human, made communing with God a priority. Jesus was properly related to God and to His friends and associates, so prayer was natural for Him. This should also be our goal. The key, however, is to get and stay in right relationship with God and others. We cannot be out of proper relationship with our brother, daughter, spouse, or coworker and expect that God will honor our prayers just the same. Instead, we will find that God will bring these unhealthy situations and relationships to our minds during our prayer time.

We can get out of right relationship by neglecting times of fellowship and communion. We can get out of right relationship by refusing to forgive or by allowing unresolved conflicts to linger. No matter what the issue is, how big or how small, it is important to remember that God is always concerned about relationship. God wants us to rightly relate to the other people in our lives. Whenever this is not the case, we can rest assured that our times of prayer will not be peaceful. The good news, however, is that the quality of our prayer life with God also affects the quality of our relationships with others. Therefore, when we come to God in prayer, we should see it as an investment into both our spiritual and human relationships.

Ultimately, building a dynamic and consistent prayer life should be high on our list of priorities. We do this because we know that prayer is purposeful; prayer has the power to change people, perspectives, and predicaments.

The LORD is far from the wicked, but He hears the prayer of the righteous. (Proverbs 15:29 HCSB)

Day 3–Learning from Our Experiences

Recall and reflect or journal about a time when you had a positive experience in prayer. How did that make you feel? Was your experience positive simply because you received something from God, or do you see how you benefited from communing with God, independent of what you "received"? What were some of those benefits?

Meditate upon the following verses and take time to thank God for desiring to meet with you in prayer. Ask God to help you increase your desire to know God through time spent in prayer. Make a list of prayer topics that can guide you during your prayer time.

Matthew 7:7–11: Keep on asking, and you will receive what you ask for. Keep on seeking, and you will find. Keep on knocking, and the door will be opened to you. For everyone who asks, receives. Everyone who seeks, finds. And to everyone who knocks, the door will be opened. You parents—if your children ask for a loaf of bread, do you give them a stone instead? Or if they ask for a fish, do you give them a snake? Of course not! So if you sinful people know how to give good gifts to your children, how much more will your heavenly Father give good gifts to those who ask him? (NLT)

Day 4—Biblical Character Reflection: Daniel

Daniel was truly a prayer warrior. Read Daniel 6, where we find the account of the persecution and trauma that Daniel endured because of his commitment to his prayer life. Through Daniel's story we can gain insight about the benefits of developing a lifestyle of prayer.

Daniel had a **pattern** of prayer in his life. Daniel's relationship with God was strong and healthy. Daniel was gifted and he received promotion, elevation, and favor with King Darius because he was a faithful follower of his God.

Daniel's lifestyle opened him up to **persecution and pain**. What we do not always realize is that when we set our minds and hearts to follow, obey, and trust God—we put a target on our backs. We get the enemy's attention when we get serious about developing and growing our relationship with Christ. This was true in Daniel's life. Daniel's enemies concocted a plan to take him out because they knew how deep and sincere his commitment was to his God. The takeaway for us from Daniel's life is that even when he was persecuted, he stayed true to his commitment and he asked God to help him. Daniel did not seek to take matters into his own hands.

Daniel was fully **persuaded** about God's character and God's ability to help him. Daniel humbly faced his lion's den, trusting and depending upon God to aid him and see him through. After his ordeal (verse 22), Daniel attributed his deliverance to God. Daniel had learned a lot about the nature and character of God during his devotion and prayer times. After his lion-den experience, Daniel was even more convinced that his God had all power and would vindicate him.

We must learn to trust God as Daniel did. We may attract unwanted attention from our enemies because of our faithful lifestyles. Nevertheless, when we remain committed and connected to God in prayer, even amid our storms, we will have the opportunity to learn more about God and experience God's abiding care in our lives.

Days 5-7—Making the Connection. Moving Forward.

This week we have sought to expand our definition and understanding of prayer. We have learned that prayer is its own reward and that the purpose of developing and maintaining a lifestyle of prayer is to draw us closer and closer to Christ.

Another beautiful thing about prayer is that even though our motivation and goal for prayer is not simply to receive from God, prayer does come with substantial results and benefits. As we close our study, let us discuss a few of the wonderful results of prayer.

Prayer encourages our focus. Prayer helps our perspective. When we pray, we can gain the proper outlook on life, on people, and on our situations. When we pray, we learn to believe and trust that God is with us and well able to help us. Life is full of ways to distract us from seeing and believing God's truth. Prayer has the power to refocus our attention back to God. Matthew 26:41 says: "Keep watch and pray, so that you will not give in to temptation. For the spirit is willing, but the body is weak!" (NLT) It takes work to keep our focus on the power and ability of Jesus. Our flesh and our heart can be fragile, causing us to doubt, that is why we need to be engaged in a lifestyle of prayer.

We can face some devastating, debilitating, and disheartening circumstances in life. Tribulations, trials, and temptations are real.

The truth is that obstacles do not wait for us to get ready; we must stay ready through cultivating a lifestyle of prayer. Prayer is empowering because it draws us closer to God. As we get closer to God, we come to understand that no matter what we are facing, no matter who comes or who goes, God is our greatest need. Cultivating a God-first mentality will help to make us prepared for whatever life may bring and encourage us to focus on the truth despite all the tricks of the enemy. We do not know what lies ahead, but God knows and God will give us the wisdom, guidance, grace, and peace we need when we pray.

I will instruct you and teach you in the way you should go; I will guide you with My eye. (Psalm 32:8 NKJV)

Prayer enlarges our faith in God. Faith or belief is what gives muscle to our prayers. According to the Life Application Study Bible, "Prayer is the key that unlocks faith in our life." (Footnote on Mark 9:29, pg. 1892) In fact, prayer leads to belief and belief leads to prayer. Whenever our belief is shaky, we know that we need to spend time with God. It is not simply that we believe or have faith that is the critical component. The key is the object of our faith: Jesus.

If we are honest, sometimes we can become intoxicated with our own level of faith and think that that is what truly matters. We must be careful, however, because the Bible says that "even the demons believe—and tremble!" (James 2:19 NKJV) If we do not stay connected to God in prayer, we can find that our faith can become anchored in things and people other than God. We must keep our focus on the God in whom we believe; not our experiences, our wishes, or even our interpretations of God's Word. We are not great because we believe; we are effective because we know *in whom* we believe and we know that God is great. We need faith and we need our works that are inspired by our faith. Nevertheless, we cannot forget that it is in Christ, not our faith, that "we live and move and exist." (Acts 17:28 NLT)

Having a lifestyle of prayer will continually bring this truth to bear in our lives. The more we pray, the more we learn about God; and the more we commune with God, the more we learn about ourselves and become convinced of our deep need for Christ. No matter how old we are, or how long we have been in relationship with God, our need for God never diminishes. Prayer keeps God on our minds. When we are thinking about God, considering who God is and what God has done, our faith in God will grow.

This I recall to my mind, therefore I have hope. Through the LORD'S mercies we are not consumed, because His compassions fail not. They are new every morning; great is Your faithfulness. (Lamentations 3:21–23 NKJV)

Prayer ensures our fruitfulness. When we are engaged in a lifestyle of prayer, we are guaranteed to be productive and fruitful. In other words, we will be able to see our obstacles removed and our enemies overcome because God responds to prayer and we gain strength to fight, push, and press on when we pray.

One test for determining the effectiveness of our prayer life is to consider what kind of results we are experiencing. There should be tangible and intangible, internal and external, immediate and long-term change in us, in our life, and in our lifestyle because of the time we spend in prayer. Our prayers should draw us closer to God. So, even if God does not change the circumstance about which we are praying, we can be changed in the midst of the circumstance. When we pray, we should expect our prayers to be fruitful and to produce results.

Jesus has given us great authority to speak and to change our lives. A grand trick of the enemy is to infiltrate our minds with hopelessness and despair. We are not defeated. We are victorious. Let us act like victors every day! Great and mighty battles are fought and won in prayer. So, let us pray!

Are any of you suffering hardships? You should pray. Are any of you happy? You should sing praises. Are any of you sick? You should call for the elders of the church to come and pray over you, anointing you with oil in the name of the Lord. Such a prayer offered in faith will heal the sick, and the Lord will make you well. And if you have committed any sins, you will be forgiven. Confess your sins to each other and pray for each other so that you may be healed. ***The earnest prayer of a righteous person has great power and produces wonderful results.*** (James 5:13–16 NLT, emphasis added)

Week 10–Relationships
Show Yourself Friendly

Week 10–Relationships
Show Yourself Friendly

The one who walks with the wise will become wise, but a companion of fools will suffer harm. (Proverbs 13:20 HCSB)

Consider carefully the company that you keep and with whom you share your dreams, visions, issues, problems, and dilemmas. Walking with those who are wise will make your life better. Walking with those who are unwise—those who consistently make choices that dishonor God and others, those who are slaves to their appetites and desires, those who always lead but submit to and follow no one—will eventually corrupt your living, thinking, and being. Be careful about the company you keep.

This is advice which we all likely received in our childhood, and its impact cannot be overstated. Most of the time, however, we are being admonished about staying out of trouble when we are told to consider the company we keep. And certainly, as today's focus text indicates, walking with those who are foolish is harmful. Nevertheless, it is critically important to think about the effect of good friends upon our lives, not just bad ones. Good friendships do not occur by happenstance. Good friendships come from the hand of God and are sustained by our effort and God's grace. When we are surrounded by good, wise, and supportive friends, we should be grateful. When we cultivate friendships with those who are loving, authentic, humble, prayerful followers of Jesus Christ, we are truly blessed. These are the types of friendships we all need in our lives. These are the types of friends that we should all endeavor to be.

This week we are going to unlock the keys to developing, maintaining, and strengthening good, godly, Christian friendships. It is necessary for us to know that even in the days and times in which we live, God is concerned about friendships. Yes, many of us are consistently out of touch and disconnected from interpersonal relationships. Yes, electronic devices have made intimacy—touch, empathy, listening, and sharing—very difficult. Nevertheless, being and having good friends is a necessity. And, developing and maintaining genuine friendships with those who can inspire, challenge, support, and hold us accountable should be an imperative for each of us. After all, Jesus calls those who are His disciples, friends. And, if it is important for Jesus to have friends, it should be important to us as well.

Friends can destroy one another, but a loving friend can stick closer than family. (Proverbs 18:24 GW)

Questions to consider: Do you consider yourself a good friend? Why or why not? How does it feel to know that Jesus considers you a friend? Are you a good friend to Christ? What aspects of Jesus' character and personality do you seek to replicate in your human friendships? What do you find difficult about building and maintaining good friendships?

Day 2–Let's Go a Little Deeper

After King Saul had finished his conversation with David, David met Jonathan, the king's son, and there was an immediate bond of love between them. Jonathan swore to be his blood brother, and sealed the pact by giving him his robe, sword, bow, and belt. (1 Samuel 18:1–4a TLB, emphasis added)

Relationships pervade our lives. As much as some people want to declare that they are self-sufficient loners, the fact of the matter is that we all need one another, and we rely upon people all throughout our lives. We rely on strangers on the road to drive safely because we put our lives in the hands of others each time we get behind the wheel of a car. We rely upon sanitation workers to haul away our trash, even though we rarely stop them to say thank you. We rely upon police and first responders to keep us safe and postal workers to bring us our mail . . . the list goes on and on. And, while we certainly may not consider these people our "friends," we must understand that being friendly is not reserved for certain people. God desires that we show ourselves friendly by the way that we live our lives each day and by how we interact with everyone with whom we come into contact. We do not know who is watching us and we can never tell just what God may be seeking to show someone else through our friendly attitude and acts of kindness.

Moreover, when we develop the characteristic of friendliness in our lives, it then becomes easier to cultivate friendships with the right people. We cannot be friends in the truest sense of the word with everyone. And, it goes without saying that friendship means something different to each of us. Even so, there are people who come into our lives and we know that they are meant to be special. We, like Jonathan and David, can develop an immediate bond of love with certain choice people along our journey.

Then there are those who become our friends because of the circumstances and people who brought us together. For example, in my own life, some of the dearest friendships that I have are with the parents of my good friends. We do not talk very often and I rarely share deeply with them. However, they have seen me grow, develop, and mature over many years. I consider them my friends because they love me, pray for me, support me, and desire God's very best for my life, and I do the same for them.

The thing is, there are core components that cut across all levels and definitions of true friends. All good, true friendships require investments, integrity, and intimacy. As we assess if we are good friends, let us consider our level of commitment and willingness to offer each of these.

Investments. Friendships can start quickly and easily as mentioned in today's biblical passage. Jonathan and David had an immediate connection; they bonded as brothers. But, their friendship became real because of the investments they made into it and into one another. One of the greatest investments that we can make into any friendships is time. When we are willing to be present with others on a consistent and persistent basis, we are showing ourselves friendly.

Integrity. Another key component to a good friendship is integrity. The fact is that we do not always share the same level of honesty with everyone. But, when it comes to true friends, truthfulness is a must. This does not simply mean not telling lies (that is obviously necessary); but more than that, integrity is seen through how we respond to conflict, how we correct one another, and whether we can genuinely celebrate our friends' achievements. The level of integrity that is shared is often an indication of the quality of a friendship.

Intimacy. No friendship can exist without trust and no trust can be built without some level of intimacy. We must be careful and guarded about those with whom we are intimate. We seem to understand this truth when it comes to physical intimacy but are not as vigilant when it comes to our minds and emotions. The power to influence is great and should not be given to very many. Intimacy requires vulnerability and it is through being vulnerable that we truly grow, learn, and develop. A lack of at least two or three relationships in which we are intimate can indicate a serious void in our lives.

It is God's desire that each of us have healthy, mature, true friendships. The foundation for cultivating such friendships is for us to make a commitment to be a good friend. Friends and friendships are a dynamic engagement. We do not just become a good friend one day and never think about it again. It is something about which we must be conscious as we live each day.

The source of strength, wisdom, and grace to be a good friend is found in Jesus Christ. He is the One who first showed Himself friendly by coming to earth to be with humanity. He sets the standard of investment, integrity, and intimacy in our lives. We can learn a lot about how to be a friend from being with and studying the life of Christ. Consequently, a quality friendship with God helps us to acquire the mettle to be a good friend to others. And, it is in our human relations that our *friendship badge* is truly earned. Just as knowledge and skill gained in a vacuum must be tested to be authentic. We cannot simply be a good friend to ourselves and to God. Only another person can declare us a bona fide, good friend.

I shall not call you servants any longer, for a servant does not share his master's confidence. No, I call you friends, now, because I have told you everything that I have heard from the Father. (John 15:15 Phillips NT)

Day 3–Learning from Our Experiences

Recall and reflect or journal about a time when you showed yourself friendly. How did it make you feel? Then, consider a time when you know that you were not a good friend. Why was that so? What did you learn from that experience? Think about the impact of a good friend upon your life. Take some time and let them know how much you value their friendship.

Meditate upon the following verses considering what it means to be a friend of Jesus. How can you improve your friendship with the Lord? Are you truly committed to obeying Jesus in every area of your life? If not, what will it take for you to make such a commitment? What does Jesus need to say or do to cause your heart to turn fully and obediently toward Him in faith? Be honest. God loves you enough to meet you where you are and walk with you to where you should be.

John 15:12–14: This is my commandment, that you love one another as I have loved you. No one has greater love than this, to lay down one's life for one's friends. You are my friends if you do what I command you. (NRSV)

Day 4–Biblical Character Reflection: Hananiah, Mishael, and Azariah (Three Hebrew Boys)

We are introduced to these three friends of Daniel in Daniel 1. It is in this first chapter that their names are changed to Shadrach, Meshach and Abednego. In Daniel 3, we read about a time of testing that these young men experienced. Their friendship shows us that standing together with others who share your beliefs and convictions can make your times of testing and trial more bearable. We also see that God not only honors our individual faith and commitment, but also God honors those things when they are shared in community.

We tend to have a very personal perspective about our faith and our relationship with Christ. One the one hand, this is good because, of course, we each must make an individual decision to call on the name of Jesus for salvation and love God. But, on the other hand, we can never truly understand ourselves or our God standing in isolation. When we elevate the personal relationship aspect of our faith, we diminish the impact of what happens, what can only happen, in community. Everything about who we are, who we think we are, and who we want to be was birthed in and through our communities (i.e., family, friends, coworkers). This is also true about how we understand God and how we express our faith.

It is detrimental to our overall growth and effectiveness in life when we do not understand that the Christian faith is intended to be lived out together with others. We may make a personal proclamation of faith, but the manifestation of our faith is very interpersonal and interdependent on others. In other words, your *personal* faith means very little unless and until you connect it with the faith of others and are required to live it out while walking, thinking, talking, and being—in community. For without a community, you do not have a way to test the depth of your faith.

We see this clearly in the story of the three Hebrew boys. The story is that King Nebuchadnezzar made a decree requiring that, at the sound of the music, everyone had to bow down to his golden image. The three Hebrew boys, who were also leaders in their community, refused to bow down and worship the king's image. They would not worship any other god but their God. They stood together and were ultimately thrown into the fire together. And, they were also delivered from that fiery furnace, together. Because of their faith and commitment to God, even the king had to declare that their God was true; their God is the only God that should be worshiped.

We can learn from these three friends that our godly convictions, faithful confessions, and overall confidence in God grows when we stand together with other believers. If it had been just one of them, standing alone, that individual may have crumbled. But, standing together, they were strong. We need to learn to develop and maintain these types of relationships in our lives. Just like a newborn baby cannot grow unless he or she is held and loved by someone else. So too it is with our faith. We need one another to grow, mature, and develop our faith.

He said to him, "'You shall love the Lord your God with all your heart, and with all your soul, and with all your mind.' This is the greatest and first commandment. And a second is like it: 'You shall love your neighbor as yourself.' On these two commandments hang all the law and the prophets." (Matthew 22:37–40 NRSV)

Days 5-7—Making the Connection. Moving Forward.

It is through this one area, the area of relationships, that we who proclaim Christ could truly transform the world. That may sound like hyperbole, but it is not. Relationships mean that much to Jesus, and God can do more through our healthy families, marriages, and friendships than through the best sermon preached by the best pastor on the perfect day. We need to be engaged in healthy, growing, and dynamic relationships and we need to be the type of friends that others want in their lives.

It is because this area is so critical to our lives that we experience so much opposition and challenge in it. Things indeed fall apart right before our eyes. What starts out with so much potential can deteriorate right within our hands. Nevertheless, we need to be diligent and vigilant about building and maintaining our relationships. It is not humanly possible to do it on our own. If we will do it, we need the grace, wisdom, strength, and love which only Jesus provides.

This week we have looked at some of the components that are required to build healthy friendships. As we move forward, let us take some time to consider the benefits of being in good, healthy friendships and showing ourselves friendly. For, even in those times when relationships are difficult, the benefits of them far outweigh the burdens.

Consider what the writer of the book of Ecclesiastes says about the benefits of friendship:

> Two people are better off than one, for they can help each other succeed. If one person falls, the other can reach out and help. But someone who falls alone is in real trouble. Likewise, two people lying close together can keep each other warm. But how can one be warm alone? A person standing alone can be attacked and defeated, but two can stand back-to-back and conquer. Three are even better, for a triple-braided cord is not easily broken. (Ecclesiastes 4:9–12 NLT)

From this passage, we can see at least four benefits of being a friend of Jesus and others:

Reward for our labor. Simply put, nine times out of ten, you get more work done and you get a greater reward when you work together with others. Even if you are not working on the same task, it has been proven that simply working with someone else in the same room or office tends to make you more productive.

When we apply this to our lives, we can see the great benefit to connecting and staying with the right people. The reward for our labor is that we build faster; we build stronger; and what we build is more sufficient when we do it together. Our strength is doubled when our strength is shared. Our world is becoming so competitive, but that should not characterize believers in Christ. We do not need to compete with one another because we know that God is faithful and has enough blessings to go around.

Moreover, we must rely upon our friendship with Jesus so that God's strength can be perfected through our weakness. When we stand alone, we often need to feign that we are self-sufficient. When we stand together, with God, we can humbly and boldly confess that our sufficiency is in Christ, the One who always has more than enough.

*And he called his twelve disciples together and began sending them out **two by two** ....* (Mark 6:7a NLT, emphasis added)

Recovery from our faults. Falling and failure are commonplace in life; getting up is not. This is partially because we do not let people know when we fall. Instead, we hide our mistakes, our shortcomings, and our failures because of shame, pride, or embarrassment. When we do this, we only hurt ourselves and prolong our pain and misery. Just because you fall does not mean that you must stay down. When you fall, literally, spiritually, financially, or even emotionally, it is good to have some friends who will help to lift you back up again. It is good to be the type of friend that helps others get back up. In fact, there is no justification for leaving someone who desires to be restored and to recover in their faults. Furthermore, even if someone is not ready when you want them to be, you should make sure they know that restoration, at least in the eyes of God, is always a possibility. (See Galatians 6:1)

Moreover, the Bible declares that if we repent our faults, failures, and sins to Christ, that He is faithful and just to forgive us and to cleanse us from all unrighteousness. (See 1 John 1:9) There is nothing—not even sin and your deliberate mistakes—which can separate you from God and keep you down, unless you let it. You can recover from your faults. Others can as well. Do it together.

[F]or though the righteous fall seven times, they rise again, but the wicked stumble when calamity strikes. (Proverbs 24:16 NIV)

Relief from the cold. Coldness in this case can be literal, spiritual, and figurative. Life, time, and chance happen to us all. When the winds of life begin to blow upon us, in the form of unemployment, death, illness, bankruptcy, setbacks, and hardships, we need not endure the cold alone. We must be alert to the fact that one of the tricks of the enemy is to isolate us during our chilly seasons. Isolation can cause us to doubt God and ourselves. When cold winds blow, our friends need us even more, not less.

The truth is, however, that drawing closer to others during hard times will be difficult, unless we have first drawn closer to God. The best security for coldness is a growing and developing relationship with God through Jesus Christ. Our times of prayer, daily devotion, worship, service, and commitment help to keep the fires of love, joy, peace, and wisdom burning. When you draw closer to God, God will give you the strength you need to stay committed to your spouse, to stay connected to that backslidden friend, to stay affirming to that coworker, and to remain supportive of that wayward child. We can all find ourselves out in the cold. But, there is no need to stay there. Relief is available.

. . . Weeping may endure for a night, but joy comes in the morning. (Psalm 30:5 NKJV)

Redemption for our lives. The Ecclesiastes text says that you need a friend to stick by you when someone (or something) more powerful than you seeks to take your life. Every now and then we all need someone who will fight for us, someone who will have our backs. Our very lives may depend upon whether or not we have some good friends and whether we have shown ourselves friendly. That is why it is so significant that we remember that Christ calls us friends. No matter what season of life you may be journeying through, there is no one better to have by your side than Jesus. You plus God is stronger than any opponent you can ever face.

We all needed a savior, and in Jesus we find just that and so much more. We could not earn our salvation, so Christ secured it for us with His own body and blood. Now, we have the choice to follow Jesus' example and stand by others and show them that in Jesus Christ, there is always hope, always help, always an offer of redemption. Having received the greatest offer of friendship ever known to humankind, how much more should we show ourselves friendly? Freely we have received. Freely let us give.

A friend loves at all times, and a brother is born for a time of adversity. (Proverbs 17:17 NIV)

Week 11—Our Thoughts
Get Your Mind Right!

Week 11–Our Thoughts
Get Your Mind Right!

You will keep the mind that is dependent on You in perfect peace, for it is trusting in You. Trust in the Lord forever, because in Yah, the Lord, is an everlasting rock! (Isaiah 26:3–4 HCSB)

Do you realize that you are engaged in warfare each day of your life? This is not a rhetorical question. Every day of your life you are engaged in a spiritual battle. If we do not remember this fact, we will be at risk for going into this battle unprepared. A lack of preparation almost always leads to defeat. We are not defeated; however, we have the victory in Jesus Christ.

The enemy is deliberate and unrelenting in the ways that he attacks our mind. Guilt, depression, anxiety, fear, worry, doubt, recalling of mistakes, shame, self-pity, and embarrassment are just some of the mental attacks with which we must contend. Nevertheless, we can overcome each attack of the enemy by exercising faith, putting on the mind of Christ, and arming ourselves for battle. This week we will focus on how to get and keep our mind properly renewed and open to the transformative power of the Holy Spirit. For, the mind is a battlefield upon which we must win.

All too often we are of the erroneous belief that we cannot help what flows in and through our mind. Not true! We can determine and set the agendas for our mind, in fact, if you are not doing so, then you should be concerned. If you are not consistently and deliberately setting the tone for your thoughts, then most likely the enemy is doing it for you.

While our minds can withstand a lot of pressure, they nevertheless are quite fragile and need to be protected and shielded from unnecessary harm. Moreover, when our mind has been injured, we need to allow it adequate time to heal. The best way to protect and guard our mind is by intentionally fixing it upon the word of God and by allowing the Holy Spirit free rein to transform our thinking to be like Christ's. This is what Paul meant when he wrote in Philippians 2:5 to "Let the same mind be in you that was in Christ Jesus." (NRSV) This is the never-ending task that is before us.

Questions to consider: What is the general tone of your thoughts? Are you a worrier? Do you consistently correct yourself and others, even in your mind? Identify at least two areas of your life about which you need to start better directing your mind. What do you honestly think about God?

Day 2—Let's Go a Little Deeper

Finally, beloved, whatever is true, whatever is honorable, whatever is just, whatever is pure, whatever is pleasing, whatever is commendable, if there is any excellence and if there is anything worthy of praise, think about these things. (Philippians 4:8 NRSV)

This passage in Philippians 4 is the basis for stating that we can set the tone and agenda for our thoughts. If we did not have the authority, by the power of the Holy Spirit working in us, to direct our thoughts, why would the Bible instruct us to do so? It is important that we be convinced that we can control our thinking, or we will not be able to apply this power to our daily lives.

The next step after believing that you can do it, is actually doing it. And, like with all things that we need to change, we must recognize what we are already doing before we can do something new. No matter how well you may feel like you are controlling your thoughts currently, you can always do better. The barrage of attacks that we receive daily requires that we keep our thought-life tight. Here is the secret. No matter how hard we try, we are not going to be able to keep the right thoughts going in and through our minds.

Our task then, is not so much to simply think the right thoughts from the outside in, but rather to draw so closely to God, that God begins to direct our thoughts from the inside out.

Here are some practical steps to set the direction of your thoughts:

Be Conscious. Become aware of what you are thinking concerning the important areas of your life. When it comes to your goals, lifestyle, dreams, relationships, affections, and most importantly God, what do you think? Take time to listen to what is playing in the background of your mind as you go about your tasks. To the extent you realize that those thoughts are negative, false, or otherwise unhelpful, determine to change them. We cannot change that which we will not acknowledge. There are clear indications given through our lives each day about what we think because it comes out in what we say and do. In fact, our behavior is a direct indication of what we believe. It is all connected, and it all begins in the mind. Be conscious of your thoughts.

Be Contemplative. After you get a glimpse into your thoughts, the next step is to understand from where the thoughts are coming. What is the source of the errant thoughts running through your mind? Is it your fear, your past experiences, your friends, or other influences? The thing is, you can easily decide to change your thinking, but unless you can stem the source of the old thoughts, you will eventually fall back into those same unhelpful mind-sets. You must redirect your mind.

To do so, you should spend time reflecting upon why your thinking is off in the first place. It could be that what you spend your time thinking about is factual and the reality of your current situation. Many people justify dwelling on negative, hurtful, and harmful stuff by saying that they are just being "real." This sounds okay, but the reality of your situation, while not to be ignored, is certainly not where your mind should be fixated. The truth of God's Word and the truth of Christ's presence and authority in our lives should outweigh even the real situations with which we are dealing. Our awareness will open the door for us to identify how our thinking needs to change. Armed with this information, we can then come up with a plan to correct it.

Our battle is to bring down every deceptive fantasy and every imposing defense that men erect against the true knowledge of God. We even fight to capture every thought until it acknowledges the authority of Christ. (2 Corinthians 10:5 Phillips NT)

Be Corrective. The last step is to correct your thinking by reassessing your circumstances and conditions through the lens of God's truth. Reassessing gives you the opportunity to balance whatever negative reality you are facing with the truth of who Christ is, what Christ has done in the past, and what Christ can do in the future. In other words, instead of dwelling on your problems, think on the promises of God.

Reassess your life and circumstances after inserting God into the center of the picture— not you, not your lack, not your current issue. If God is the source of your hope, you will never be disappointed. (See Romans 5) Learn to say "so what" to all the bad reports and lies that come from your enemies. Become proficient at using "the sword of the Spirit which is the word of God" to correct your thinking. (Ephesians 6:17 NKJV) Find promises and truths in God's Word and apply them to your life. Do not simply accept whatever your mind thinks. Get your mind right!

Day 3–Learning from Our Experiences

Recall and reflect or journal about what you are learning this week about your thought-life. The truth of the matter is that it is very hard to capture each thought that goes through our mind. What we need to be more conscious about, however, are the thoughts that come up again and again. About what do you ruminate? Are you rehashing bad experiences, mistakes, or shortcomings of yourself and others? Are you continuously recalling what bad things others have said or done to you, or where you missed the mark?

These are the thoughts we must work to change. What you dwell upon becomes what you believe. What you believe, you will eventually say. What you say becomes your actions. What you continuously do becomes your lifestyle. Stop those bad thoughts before they infect your entire life.

Meditate upon the following verses thanking God for the power and authority you have been given to set the tone for your thoughts. Forgive yourself for where you have missed the mark and decide today to start thinking better about yourself, about others, and most importantly about Jesus Christ. The truth is, when you are in Christ, you are never defeated, unless of course, you think that you are.

2 Corinthians 4:8–10: We are pressed on every side by troubles, but we are not crushed. We are perplexed, but not driven to despair. We are hunted down, but never abandoned by God. We get knocked down, but we are not destroyed. Through suffering, our bodies continue to share in the death of Jesus so that the life of Jesus may also be seen in our bodies. (NLT)

Romans 8:38–39: And I am convinced that nothing can ever separate us from God's love. Neither death nor life, neither angels nor demons, neither our fears for today nor our worries about tomorrow—not even the powers of hell can separate us from God's love. No power in the sky above or in the earth below—indeed, nothing in all creation will ever be able to separate us from the love of God that is revealed in Christ Jesus our Lord. (NLT)

Day 4–Biblical Character Reflection: Compilation

There is not one biblical character being highlighted this week, but many. In fact, you should take some time today to consider a biblical figure that you like and take a closer look at their story. When it comes to our thinking, no one else will know exactly what is going on inside of our heads, but eventually our thoughts will spill over into our living. When we see a man or woman in the Bible who was successful, faithful, able to overcome and endure, we know that they had God's help in setting the tone for their mind. If their mind was not set on God, God's words, and God's truth, they would have surely fallen prey to the tricks and attacks of their enemies.

Two people whose lives and stories are good for consideration on this topic are Hannah (1 Samuel 1–2:21) and Joshua (Joshua 1). Both individuals have compelling stories. They both had to deal with disappointment, doubt, and great mental pressure. Ultimately, both Hannah and Joshua displayed great faith and left a positive legacy for those who came after them. They had to keep their minds stayed on God. They had to believe that God was for them and not against them. They had to believe that all things were working together for their good, even when all they could see was evidence to the contrary. By considering their stories, we can be inspired to do the same. And, in addition to these two, take some time to consider who in your life inspires you in a similar way.

Days 5-7—Making the Connection. Moving Forward.

Do not be conformed to this world, but be transformed by the renewing of your minds, so that you may discern what is the will of God—what is good and acceptable and perfect. (Romans 12:2 NRSV)

Our mental attitudes and thoughts impact every area of our lives. It has been said that whether you think you can or you think you can't, you are right. Thinking precedes doing, so we must be deliberate about the thoughts we allow in and through our mind. The greatest sin that we commit is thinking about God in the wrong way; having the wrong perspective and attitude about God affects us more than anything else. For, how we think about God will ultimately determine how we think about ourselves and others. When you allow God to heal your mind and allow the Holy Spirit to transform your thinking, by grace, you can adjust, modify, change, improve, and better yourself and everything in your life.

This week we have learned that we have the authority and power to set the tone for our thoughts. We need not be victims to the random, wrong, and harmful thoughts that the enemy sends our way. As we move forward, the challenge before us is to truly change our thinking for the better. It may take some time, but the investment will be well worth it in the end. Remember, as you think in your heart, so are you. (See Proverbs 23:7) So, no matter what else you may do, please get your mind right!

Here is a process that you can prayerfully undertake to set the right tone and agenda for your mind each day.

Decide. The choice is yours as to the thoughts in your mind. Decide that you will forget some things from your past. Those things which are not serving you any good and not carrying you toward your desired future must be discarded. We will visit the idea of our authority again when we talk about our words because they are both so interconnected. What you must understand is that not choosing is making a choice. Meaningful change is possible. It starts with making one choice. That is, the decision to think differently.

We cannot make decisions in isolation, however. We must consult God and be honest with the godly women and men who are in our lives. Most of the time, we do not completely know what we should want or how we should think, so we need God to help us. God is always willing to do just that.

For it is God who is working in you, enabling you both to desire and to work out His good purpose. (Philippians 2:13 HCSB)

Direct. Once we determine that we will think better, then we must be deliberate and vigilant about directing our thinking moment by moment each day. The best and most effective way to direct our thoughts is by drenching our mind in God's Word. This comes through Bible study, prayer, and even music. In fact, as many times and ways that we can reinforce the truth of God's Word in our mind, the better.

I will never forget visiting a woman who had battled sickness for many years, just days before she transitioned to be with the Lord. I was overwhelmed by the calm peacefulness of her home.

I was also amazed to see these little post-it notes that she had on the walls. They were in her bedroom, bathroom, and kitchen. The post-it notes had Bible verses, positive quotes, and affirmations written on them. She did this to direct her thoughts. No matter how she may have felt in her body on any given day, she knew that what she believed in her mind was more important. She was a very wise woman.

It takes wisdom, discipline, and faith to redirect our minds away from the facts and toward the truth of God's Word. Nevertheless, it can be done. The facts are real, but the power of Jesus Christ to change, alter, and modify our reality, in a matter of moments, is always more real. Moreover, even if our circumstances do not change as we hope, God has the power to sustain and uphold us. This is the truth upon which we must learn to dwell.

Decree. The only thing left to do after we decide and begin to direct our thoughts is to declare and decree what is in our mind. What we believe to be true, we say. Our declarations of faith go a long way to keeping our minds convinced of God's truth. It is not enough to know a few verses from the Bible; to fully activate the power of God's Word in our lives, we must declare, decree, and speak what we know.

Furthermore, we should continuously seek out the truth about God, so that we can declare it as well. This is not something we do one time and never do again. It must become our pattern to think right and then say what we think. Your words have power, and life and death come through your tongue. (See Proverbs 18:21)

*He said to them, "Because of your little faith. For truly I tell you, if you have faith the size of a mustard seed, you will **say** to this mountain, 'Move from here to there,' and it will move; and nothing will be impossible for you."* (Matthew 17:20 NRSV, emphasis added)

Week 12–The Power of Words
What Are You Saying?!?!

Week 12–The Power of Words
What Are You Saying?!?!

Words kill, words give life; they're either poison or fruit—you choose.
(Proverbs 18:21 MSG)

What is the soundtrack of your life? What are the themes, topics, experiences, and memories that are constantly going through your mind, and finding their way out of your mouth? If you don't know, you may want to find out, and soon. For you see, our words are a compass. They quickly reveal not only where we are, but also where we are going. Whether we want to believe it or not, our words have power. Moreover, our words expose the quality and condition of our hearts. For, "the mouth speaks the things that are in the heart." (Matthew 12:34b NCV)

I'll be the first to admit that I am a lover of words. Words make me happy, except when they do not. And, I'm becoming increasingly unhappy about the way that too many of us use our words against ourselves and against others. The longer that I live, the more it becomes clear that the writer of Proverbs chapter 18 is right. Words either kill or they give life; and the choice as to what will be the effect of my words is all mine.

The number of things, people, and situations in our lives and world over which we have utterly no control could never be counted. Yet, one thing which we absolutely can command is our tongue. Nevertheless, this is an area where many of us struggle. Instead of using our wise minds and sincere hearts to dominate our tongues and dictate the course of our lives, more and more we are being dominated by our tongues. It is not true that our words are all that matter; for our words are based upon our thinking and heart attitude. We all say things in jest or sarcastically from time to time, which do not have the passion and true meaning behind them. Nevertheless, what comes out of our mouths on a consistent basis reveals more about us than we may realize.

You may be thinking, *yes, words are important*, but actions speak louder than words. The truth is, however, that our actions are the words that we have already spoken. We will never do the things that we say we cannot do. We will never become the people that we declare that we cannot (or will not) become. Thus, it would behoove us to get command of our tongues before the chaos, addiction, and destruction that our mouths help to create is manifested. Do not delay because by the time that your words become actions, it will likely be too late.

This week we will seek to get a command on just what we are saying. The goal of doing this is to develop a new appreciation, respect, and understanding for the power of our words. Learning to be more cautious, considerate, and careful about the words that you think and say will impact every area of your life. Once you realize the power of your words, you will also know that whatever you want to create, change, or cease in your life can and will be done with your words.

Questions to consider: What is the soundtrack of your life? What words are you repeating over and over to yourself and to others? On a day-to-day basis, what are you consuming the most through your eyes and ears? Is it the word of God (through music, reading, and study), television, celebrity gossip, music, conversations with others, or something else? Ask God to help you to hear what you are saying over the next week.

Day 2–Let's Go a Little Deeper

We all make many mistakes. If people never said anything wrong, they would be perfect and able to control their entire selves, too. (James 3:2 NCV)

Speaking right and well on a consistent basis is no easy task. There are so many temptations, which beckon us to misuse the power of our words. Knowing this, it should be our goal to allow the Holy Spirit to develop within us a pattern of being cautious and careful with our words. We will not be able to do this on our own, but if we are open to the Spirit's movement in our hearts, we can learn to speak what is right and pleasing to God.

The fact is, our words give great insight and are a clear indication of what is going on inside of us. As the passage quoted above from James states, when someone controls their tongue, we know that they can control every other part of their life as well. The opposite is also true. Those of us who refuse to get a handle on how we use our words will have a hard time reigning in other areas of our lives. Lest we think this is no big deal, consider the strong word of warning that Jesus spoke to the religious leaders of His day about the source of words and being held accountable for what we say. The following is recorded in Matthew 12:34–37:

> You snakes! You are evil people, so how can you say anything good? The mouth speaks the things that are in the heart. Good people have good things in their hearts, and so they say good things. But evil people have evil in their hearts, so they say evil things. And I tell you that on the Judgment Day people will be responsible for every careless thing they have said. The words you have said will be used to judge you. Some of your words will prove you right, but some of your words will prove you guilty. (NCV)

This passage is too important to be disregarded. Our response to it, however, should not only be to feel remorseful about how we may have used our words in the past, but also to feel empowered to make positive change. By drawing closer to God in prayer and devotion, we can have our hearts cleaned, healed, and made right. (See John 15:3) When our hearts are right, our words will fall in line. We can change with God's help and God is always available and willing to help us. Here are three practical steps to keep in mind to tame the tongue:

Pause. Listen to your words. Reflect upon your words. Be more careful. Having a sense of personal awareness helps in making necessary changes. Train your tongue to wait before it speaks. Remember, "Those who are careful about what they say protect their lives, but whoever speaks without thinking will be ruined." (Proverbs 13:3 NCV)

Practice. Change takes an investment of time and energy. If you find that your words are not what they should be, be kind to yourself about it. Extend grace inward. God does not condemn you, do not condemn yourself. God wants to unleash the power within you to be and do better. Practice self-love. Moreover, practice self-control.

Most of the time, we misspeak out of anger, frustration, pain, or even fear. Reclaim your personal authority by submitting yourself to God and allowing the Holy Spirit to help you develop new patterns and forge new pathways with your words. Practice may not literally make you perfect, but, it certainly will not hurt.

Pray. Ask for help. Oftentimes we are oblivious to our habits of speaking and being. Like asking fish to recognize water, asking us to see our faults and inconsistencies and to hear our own broken soundtrack is very, very hard. Nevertheless, we are not alone. Jesus is available and able to guide us, if we will only ask. So, pray and ask the Lord to reveal to you any areas where you are speaking death instead of life. Moreover, ask your close friends and loved ones to help you and hold you accountable. Be open to feedback and willing to change.

Stay awake and pray for strength against temptation. The spirit wants to do what is right, but the body is weak. (Mark 14:38 NCV)

Day 3—Learning from Our Experiences

Recall and reflect or journal about a time when your words got you in trouble. How did you recover? Consider a time when someone else's words hurt you deeply. How did you handle the situation? Did being on the receiving end of unkind words help you to better appreciate the impact of your own words upon others? Reflect also upon a time when you used your words to speak life to a person or situation. How did that make you feel?

Meditate upon the following verses asking God to give you a heart of forgiveness toward those who have spoken carelessly to you. Moreover, ask Jesus to show you a person in your life to whom you need to speak better. Start using your words to build that person up today. The person may very well be you!

Ephesians 4:29–32: Do not let any unwholesome talk come out of your mouths, but only what is helpful for building others up according to their needs, that it may benefit those who listen. And do not grieve the Holy Spirit of God, with whom you were sealed for the day of redemption. Get rid of all bitterness, rage and anger, brawling and slander, along with every form of malice. Be kind and compassionate to one another, forgiving each other, just as in Christ God forgave you. (NIV)

Day 4—Biblical Character Reflection: The Shunammite Woman

We can read the Shunammite woman's story in 2 Kings 4:8–37. She was a faithful, kindhearted, and compassionate woman who befriended the prophet Elisha. She had a special room prepared in her home for the prophet to stay whenever he visited the town of Shunem. She shows us the benefit of having a clean heart toward God and the people of God and how your heart will direct your words, even in the most difficult of circumstances.

As the story goes, Elisha comes to the woman one evening and asks her how he can repay her for her generosity and kindness toward him. (See verse 13) The woman, however, does not utter a request or a complaint about anything in her life to the prophet.

This is an indication about the attitude of her heart. First, she had not been kind to Elisha simply because she wanted something in return. She did not go to him to ask for anything; instead, he came to her to ask what he could do.

Second, even when he asked her what she needed, she still did not complain. There are many reasons why this may have been. Perhaps she was truly at peace or perhaps she did not believe that Elisha could change her situation. Nevertheless, it is revealed to us that the woman is barren and without a son. Elisha says to her that she will bear a son and give birth in about a year. (See verse 15) She had not asked, yet Elisha grants what is most likely the deepest desire of her heart. We can learn from her experience. She became pregnant and had a son just as Elisha had spoken.

Tragically, however, the boy dies one day after a brief time of illness. It is at this point in the story that we truly see the heart and faith of the Shunammite woman. When her son dies, she does not curse God or Elisha. She does not cry. She does not complain. She takes the boy up to Elisha's little room, places him on the bed, and then sets off to go to the prophet, who is currently in another town. This woman knew that she had to take her problem to the one who had given her the gift. In this case, Elisha stood in the place of God. In our lives, we too must learn to first take our problems to the giver of every good and perfect gift—God. We can complain to others, but only the God who gave us the child, spouse, job, or home will be able to give us the wisdom we need to care for it.

The woman sets off to go to Elisha and she does not utter a word of her son's death to anyone; not her husband, not her driver, and not even to Elisha's servant (Gehazi) when he meets her on the road. In fact, when asked by Gehazi if everything is well or at peace, she responds, "It is well." (Verse 26) It is not until she gets to Elisha that she starts to reveal the pain, dismay, and distress within her heart. She reveals this to Elisha because he can handle it. God can handle our emotions—including disappointment and pain.

The story ends with Elisha coming to the aid of the boy and, ultimately, after Elisha prays and breathes on him, the boy is revived. Elisha gives her a son again.

The Shunammite woman was not super human. She did not ignore the pain or disappointment of her circumstance, but she also did not speak death to an already bad situation. From her story, we can learn that when we trust completely in the Lord, the Holy Spirit will guide our words to speak peace, even in traumatic situations. Her story reminds us that God hears even the silent cries of our hearts and that God responds to our faithfulness. God can grant us even those desires that we never vocalize. God can be trusted. The question is, "Can God trust us to live in ways that honor God's Word and testify to God's faithfulness?" Furthermore, can we be trusted to speak words of faith, or will we simply articulate our fears and experiences?

What else stands out to you from the Shunammite woman's story?

Days 5-7–Making the Connection. Moving Forward.

With our tongues we bless God our Father; with the same tongues we curse the very men and women [made in God's] image. Curses and blessings out of the same mouth! My friends, this can't go on. (James 3:9–10 MSG)

We do not have to look very far to see the impact of destructive words upon our lives, homes, communities, and world. Nevertheless, we can make things different, one word at a time. This week we have learned that our words have great power and we have seen through scripture how important it is that we set our hearts and words right before God. Changing our speaking habits will not be easy or pain free; but change is possible.

We should understand at least two things about the nature of change. First, to truly change, we must be willing not only to remove bad or unproductive habits, but also to add new and healthy ones. Second, change is rarely about our willpower and personal strength. We need the help of the Holy Spirit to recognize our need to change and we need the Spirit's power to energize us to make change a reality. This is also true about changing our words. Many of us are conscious about not saying certain things, especially to certain people or in certain places. Nevertheless, we are not as careful about making sure that we say the right things.

As you move forward, the challenge is to replace or exchange your bad speaking habits with good ones. Therefore, commit yourself to do the following, with God's help:

Replace talking about your problems with confessing God's promises. Search the Bible and find a promise that relates to every problem and pain area in your life. Then, start confessing what God's Word says instead of continuously mentioning your problem. Your problem could be a health challenge, financial burden, relationship issue, or some other lack. Your problem is real, yet the word of God is true. God's truth is greater than the facts of our lives and circumstances. Dwelling only upon your difficulties will produce pain, regret, fear, and stagnation. Meditating upon the words and promises of the Lord will empower you. Use your tongue to declare God's promises, not merely to discuss your problems.

The Spirit gives life; the flesh counts for nothing. The words I have spoken to you are spirit and they are life. (John 6:63 NIV)

Replace repetitive proclamations about your experiences with professions of your expectations. We must be careful about rehearsing our sad experiences over and over again. This does not mean that we deny where we have been or what we have endured, but rather that we put greater emphasis upon where we are going. When you talk to God, yourself, and others, why not mention your great expectations, not just your bad experiences? When you continuously talk about what you have experienced, you can falsely start to believe that what has been is all that will ever be. Our experiences are not greater than God. Learn to express your expectations about God and see if God does not meet and even exceed them.

I would have lost heart, unless I had believed that I would see the goodness of the LORD in the land of the living. (Psalm 27:13 NKJV)

Replace stories about what others have done *to* you with testimonies about what God has done *for* you. We have all found ourselves on the receiving end of unkindness, pain, and stinginess. We have been betrayed, had our hearts broken and our minds manipulated. Nevertheless, telling the stories of what horrible things people have done to us does very little to keep our hearts clean and our minds focused on God's truth and goodness. Contrarily, there is great power in our testimonies of what God has done in and through our lives. These are the stories that should fill our mouths and hearts. Whenever you get the chance, draw attention to God. Point others to Christ's goodness, faithfulness, and strength. Yes, every now and then pain, problems, setbacks, and set-ups may come, but *every* day God is a keeper; God is a healer; God is faithful; and God is worthy of your praise. Run and tell that!

They triumphed over him by the blood of the Lamb and by the word of their testimony . . . (Revelation 12:11 NIV)

Week 13—Our Behavior
Do the Right Thing!

Week 13—Our Behavior
Do the Right Thing!

. . . for it is God who works in you both to will and to do for [God's] good pleasure. (Philippians 2:13 NKJV)

The past two weeks have set the groundwork for this week's topic of study: our behavior. At the end of the day, after we set our minds on what is true and right, and after we have tamed our tongues so that we speak careful and deliberate words, the only thing left is our actions. In fact, after we set our thoughts and words, our actions will fall in order. Remember, our beliefs become our thoughts. Thoughts become words. Words become actions. Actions become our lifestyle. It is a process. And, it is impossible to disconnect one aspect of our lives from the others.

Of course, each aspect of our living—thinking, speaking, and doing—will require our on-going attention and time. We will never arrive at a place where we simply do not have to watch our tongues or fortify our minds. No, as long as we are human and live on earth with other humans, perfecting our thoughts, words, and behavior will be accomplished through trial and error. Some days we will do better than others. But, as Don Miguel Ruiz expresses in his wonderful book, *The Four Agreements: A Practical Guide to Personal Freedom*, our task is to always do our best. As we press on, setting our heart and mind upon the God in whose image we are made, we will find that thinking, speaking, and acting in ways that honor God become more a part of our lifestyle each day. We cannot do it without the power of Jesus Christ operating in our lives, but with God, all things are indeed possible. (See Matthew 19:26)

The truth is, God made us and calls us to a certain standard in how we live. God's standard is clear and nonnegotiable:

> But be holy in all you do, just as God, the One who called you, is holy. It is written in the Scriptures: "You must be holy, because I am holy." (1 Peter 1:15–16 NCV)

The standard of God is holiness in every manner of our living, moving, and being. We will spend time tomorrow delving more deeply into the idea of holiness, but for now just understand that God is concerned about ensuring that we act in ways that honor God. God wants us to live like Jesus Christ. Because, like it or not, the behavior (responses, reactions, choices) of believers of Christ make a difference in how God is viewed by the world in which we live. The world needs to see and know God to be redeemed, so we must be the hands, feet, and mouthpieces of Jesus.

The question for us to wrestle with this week is, "What does how you behave—on a consistent basis—say about your relationship with Jesus and about God?" We must answer this question as individuals and then we must consider it as the collective Body of Christ. As members of the Body, we do not get to pick and choose which of our actions impacts and affects the other members. We are connected and we help or hurt one another by the things we say and do. We are a package deal. This is important because sometimes your choice to modify your behavior will be motivated not by what you *feel* like doing, but rather by what you *understand* is best for those to whom you are connected. The good news is that as we grow in Christ and learn more about God's character, credibility, and conduct, we will have all the motivation that we need to allow God to work in us to "will and to do of [God's] good pleasure." (Philippians 2:13 NKJV) By God's grace and through the power of the Holy Spirit, God can make us better and empower us to be our very best selves.

Don't you realize that all of you together are the temple of God and that the Spirit of God lives in you? God will destroy anyone who de-

*stroys this temple. For God's temple is holy, and **you are that temple**.* (1 Corinthians 3:16–17 NLT, emphasis added)

Questions to consider: Are there any current behaviors that you need to change? If so, what are they? What thoughts come to mind when you consider God's instruction to be holy? What does holiness look like to you? What is your current process for controlling your behavior? Give an honest assessment of yourself; how well do you represent Christ from day to day? What do you do well? How could you be better?

Day 2—Let's Go a Little Deeper

You should know that your body is a temple for the Holy Spirit who is in you. You have received the Holy Spirit from God. So you do not belong to yourselves, because you were bought by God for a price. So honor God with your bodies. (1 Corinthians 6:19–20 NCV, emphasis added)

Honoring God with our bodies is not intended to be a burden. Our perspective should be that, considering what God has done and is doing for us, it is our humble pleasure and delight to give God glory in and through our bodies. God sent Jesus as a ransom to buy us back from defeat, death, and destruction. Anything we do is in response to Christ's sacrifice for us. It shows our appreciation and gratitude when we give ourselves fully to God, as a vessel and representative of God's goodness, kindness, love, and holiness.

Indeed, living a holy lifestyle is the natural outgrowth of having the Holy Spirit living within us. We are the house where the Holy Spirit resides; thus, holiness should be a prime characteristic of our lives. Holiness in its simplest understanding means to be set apart for God's use. Holiness is not a thing we do; it is who we are because of God's Spirit within us. We do not make ourselves holy; Jesus made us holy when He bought us with His life on the cross. Moreover, after redeeming us, Christ then brought us back to complete relationship with God, our Creator. The same Spirit that empowered Christ to do this work is ready and willing to work in our lives each day.

The picture is like one of a special dish or utensil that does not get stored in the regular kitchen cabinet but is housed in a nice display case. Moreover, while everyone can see it, not everyone can touch or use it. Only the owner has complete and intimate access to it. This is the way that Paul describes us as believers in Christ in 1 Corinthians 6:19–20 quoted above. We are not our own. We cannot act like everyone else acts because God sent Jesus to purchase us. So now, we get to be the home of the Holy Spirit of God and go the places where God takes us and act like God wants us to act. Holiness means we are special to God. We are on assignment and display for God, and God wants us to shine.

When we think about how to walk out holiness in our daily lives, one way to approach it is to commit ourselves to always be in position for God to use us. This means that we are committed to stay in such condition, that whenever Christ calls us to represent Him, there will be no barriers or prohibitions to us doing so immediately. There are at least two critical tools that have been given to us to stay in fit spiritual (and physical) condition:

The Word of God. It is through constant reading and meditating upon the word of God that we learn God's standards and understand how God wants to use our lives. The word of God is a tool to get us to the heart of God. God is not a brutal taskmaster that is only concerned about the output of your life; God is genuinely concerned about you. When we come to the word of God, we should come as a loved child comes to hang out with her mother or father; not as a fearful, timid subject comes to a harsh ruler.

Coming into the presence of God should delight us because we know that God wants us to get life right. God wants to use us in ways we have never imagined to represent the truth of Jesus Christ to the world around us. Yes, the word of God has instructions and we should be sincere and serious about learning and obeying them. Nevertheless, those instructions are good for us and much better than anything we could come up with on our own. Use the word of God to guide you to the heart of God, believing that God's heart toward you is always good.

Your word is a lamp to my feet and a light for my path. (Psalm 119:105 NIV)

The Wisdom of God. The wisdom of God is also found in God's Word, but more than that, God's wisdom is found along the path of walking with others who know God and are following Christ's great example. God's wisdom is helpful for us, but not unless and until we exercise it. We cannot become wise sitting on the bench. We cannot become wise by simply filling our heads with Scriptures, knowledge, and Bible stories. We become wise through the process of walking out our salvation (alongside others) in daily life. Going back to the idea of trial and error, we can find strength to keep walking in God's Word, not only by reading it, but also by applying it and seeing that it works.

I remember years ago, I had a situation where I was offended by a brother with whom I attended church. He spoke harshly and unkindly to me for no reason and I was hurt. I had read about what to do when offended by a fellow believer in Matthew 18. Now I had the choice to put it into practice or not. I decided to give it a try. I went to him and told him that his words had hurt me. He listened and received me with humility, acknowledged his wrong, and apologized. I forgave him and we walked forward together, reconciled. It was a watershed moment in my faith-life because I had put God's Word to the test and found it to be useful, helpful, and right. It was not necessarily what I wanted to do, but because I yielded to God's wisdom and not my own, we were all made better and God was glorified. Let the word and wisdom of God guide your heart and actions today and every day.

Getting wisdom is the wisest thing you can do! And whatever else you do, develop good judgment. (Proverbs 4:7 NLT)

Day 3–Learning from Our Experiences

Recall and reflect or journal about a time when your behavior fell short of what you know would have been God-honoring. How did you feel? What ways did you modify your thinking and behavior after that experience? What about a time when you know you represented God well; how did that make you feel?

Meditate upon the following verses. Pray and thank God for choosing you and seeing you as holy, not because of you, but because of what Jesus has done for you. What tangible ways can you respond to God's choice of you? What new ways can you praise Christ for His sacrifice through your daily living, speaking, and being?

Ephesians 1:3–6: All praise to God, the Father of our Lord Jesus Christ, who has blessed us with every spiritual blessing in the heavenly realms because we are united with Christ. Even before [God] made the world, God loved us and chose us in Christ to be holy and without fault in [God's] eyes. God decided in advance to adopt us into [God's] own family by bringing us to [God] through Jesus Christ. This is what [God] wanted to do, and it gave [God] great pleasure. So, we praise God for the glorious grace [God] has poured out on us who belong to [God's] dear Son. (NLT, emphasis added)

Day 4–Biblical Character Reflection: Queen Vashti

Queen Vashti's story is found in Esther chapter 1. She was married to King Xerxes and was deposed as queen after she refused to appear before the king when he called for her. The biblical text indicates that the king was drunk and feeling good after days of partying. He called for Queen Vashti to come before him because ". . . He wanted the nobles and all the other men to gaze on her beauty, for she was a very beautiful woman." (Esther 1:11 NLT) When Vashti refused to come, the king was both embarrassed and incensed.

It is not explicitly clear from the text why Queen Vashti refused to come when the king called. Nevertheless, we can learn some lessons to inform our behavior from Vashti's actions, even if we do not necessarily know her motivation. Vashti stood by her convictions. She refused to allow herself to be subjected to the ogling of intoxicated men, perhaps because she felt that only her husband should have that privilege, or maybe because she felt like she was worth more. Vashti does not profess to make her stand because of God; nonetheless, she shows us that doing the right thing is good in and of itself.

Vashti stood up to a powerful man, albeit her husband, whom she knew had the authority to remove her as queen. It is unlikely that she expected the king to become so angry that he would remove her, but she did what she felt was right in that instance. It is interesting to note that King Xerxes was remorseful about harkening to the voice of his advisers, which led him to make the harsh decision to banish Queen Vashti, but it was already too late. (See Esther 2:1) This serves as a reminder that we do not always get a second chance. Care and concern should be given to being led by the Holy Spirit because when we allow the voices of others to take the place of God, we will be disappointed.

We can glean some insight into doing the right thing from Vashti's story. Here are a few:

1. Doing the right thing and representing God will not always be easy.
2. Representing God will always have consequences, but we must remember that God rewards those who diligently seek God. (See Hebrews 11:6)
3. We may not know what our example will mean either to those who see it now or to those who will hear about it later but know that someone is always watching.

Vashti's story is in the Bible because her removal paved the way for Esther to become queen. Esther was able to save the Jews who were living under King Xerxes' rule because she too courageously stood up to power. Vashti did what was right and, even though it cost her her position, she set an example for the next woman in line. Our actions have an impact. By God's help, let us always endeavor that our impact be godly and positive.

It may seem that Vashti's story ends badly but consider another perspective. Yes, Vashti was removed from her position, but she retained much more. She held on to her dignity, self-respect, and personal authority. Her story is here for all of us to see that sometimes doing what is right will bring backlash and strife. Nevertheless, when we take a stand for God by faith, and when we trust the promises of Jesus Christ, we have the assurance of ultimate victory. In the short run we may lose some things by choosing to do life on God's terms, but in the long run we gain so much more and our legacy and example just may live on forever.

So, then, brothers and sisters, don't let anyone move you off the foundation [of your faith]. Always excel in the work you do for the Lord. You know that the hard work you do for the Lord is not pointless. (1 Corinthians 15:58 GW)

Days 5-7—Making the Connection. Moving Forward.

Do not offer any part of yourself to sin as an instrument of wickedness, but rather offer yourselves to God as those who have been brought from death to life; and offer every part of yourself to [God] as an instrument of righteousness. (Romans 6:13 NIV)

This week's study has focused upon our behavior, which is critically important. Nevertheless, as we finish out the week, it is necessary to remind you that belief dictates behavior. Holiness, purity, honesty, chastity, integrity, morality, and ethics all come from within us. The internal elements of your spiritual life are the external building blocks of your physical life. We express our beliefs through how we live. God asks us to live in a way that is God-honoring. Nevertheless, we cannot honor God per our own standards; we must live in obedience to the standards of Jesus Christ. This means that to honor God, we must first know God. Knowing God and trusting that Jesus is who God says Jesus is, is our highest calling and should be the greatest desire of our lives.

We must remember that our actions flow from our hearts. Furthermore, Christ is the One who redeems and restores our hearts to the place where they can honor and love God as initially intended. In other words, we do not empower ourselves to honor God, we allow God to empower us as needed. Each day we will stumble upon temptations and enticements that seek to draw us away from knowing God. These things will invite us to *figure* things out on our own, using our minds. We must resist this temptation and instead conform our thinking, being, and living to be like that of our big brother Jesus Christ. It is this daily transformation that is the key. (See Romans 12:2)

Only God has the power to transform us and to help us to live like Jesus. And, our life example is the only way that some people will come to know who God is and to understand what it looks like to be saved, sanctified, and used in service by Jesus Christ. What is equally important, however, is that with the focus on behavior, we never forget that *we are not what we do*! No matter how well or poorly we may perform, we are never our actions. We are who we are, and our actions are the products of our beliefs, thoughts, and words. Behavior and performance should never be the focus in your life. The heart of the matter with God is the matter of your heart. You are not what you do; you are who you are, and when you are in Christ, you are never held to your old behaviors because God is remaking you each day.

Consider three aspects of your life as points of focus to help you develop a lifestyle that is God-pleasing and God-honoring. If we continuously walk authentically, seeking to uphold biblical standards in these areas, then we will always be moving closer to Christ through how we live.

Practices. Everything that we want to do well, we must practice. It is an adage, but nonetheless true; practice makes perfect.

Said another way, that which we practice, we will come to do perfectly. Thus, it would be prudent of us to make sure that we practice, or do continually, only what we want to perfect in our lives. Our natural talents are perfected and strengthened through practice. However, if a naturally talented baseball player has bad form that is never corrected, he or she will simply perfect their bad form. Similarly, when it comes to developing spiritual strength, we should practice spiritual disciplines, such as worship, Bible study, prayer, and fellowship. We must do these repeatedly. Spiritual disciplines are not always fun and easy, but we must keep practicing. Failing to perfect our spiritual disciplines is akin to practicing with bad form. Eventually, our neglect will catch up with us, and quite possibly, when the game is on the line.

Understand this: obedience is hard. It is much easier to lie when convenient than to tell the truth in love. It is uncomfortable to stand out in the crowd, but that may be the place God has assigned for you to be in that moment. God may want to use your life to show those around you a truth about who God is; practice being obedient even when it is not comfortable. What you practice, you will perfect.

You will not grow spiritually strong by accident. Spiritual growth is the result of deliberate attention given to the spiritual aspects of your life. As you cultivate your spiritual relationship with Christ, your behaviors will be modified. But, it will not occur haphazardly. Growth happens on purpose. Set your mind to it. (Read Colossians 3:5–17)

People. Not only does spiritual growth not happen by accident, but moreover, it does not happen when we walk alone. We need people. People are the best and worst thing about life sometimes; nevertheless, we must keep choosing to stay connected to the right people. When we are disconnected from God, we can more easily become disconnected from people and vice versa. And, when we stay connected to God, God will show us the people with whom we have been assigned to journey in life. Whatever you think you can do alone, you can do it better and faster together with someone else.

Being and staying connected to the right people will take us toward God; the opposite is also true. Another adage that can help us on this point is that bad company does in fact spoil good morals. Oftentimes we think that we are stronger than we are. We are not. If you harken to the opinions of those who do not care about the opinion of your God, you are setting yourself up for failure. Yes, you can and should develop friendships with those who do not share your same religious or spiritual background and foundation. But no, you should not let those who are not attentive and alert to Christ's wisdom guide your life and thinking.

You should not model your behavior after or let your responses be dictated by people for whom Jesus Christ is not the standard. It may seem harsh, but this decision could be the subtle difference between ultimate success and utter setback in your life. The expectations and attitudes of those with whom we walk the closest in life will impact our perspective the most. Be careful to stay connected to the right people and be okay with allowing distance between yourself and those who mean you no good, literally and spiritually.

We each need a person to fill the following roles in our lives. You need someone who will pray for you and cry with you. You need someone who loves you enough to hold you accountable, someone who will correct you when you are wrong, and encourage you when you are right. You need someone who does not mind disagreeing with you, but who knows how to disagree without being disagreeable. You need someone who believes in you, not because of what you do, but because of who you are, and someone who will not be discouraged by your disappointments. You need someone with whom you can laugh hysterically and dream outlandishly. You need someone whose voice can calm you down and someone whose voice will lift you up. You need people who have known you and seen you grow over time, and you constantly need those who have a fresh and new perspective on you. If you pray and are open,

God will show you the right people to whom you should be connected. Trust God to do this and obey God's leading. (See Psalm 1)

Priorities. Many times in life, we miss the mark of God, not because we do not sincerely want to please Jesus, but rather because we do not prioritize. Priorities set the agenda for our day and priorities set the agenda for our lives. Many well-meaning Christians have died and gone to heaven, leaving undone and unsaid, words and deeds that would have pleased God. Time waits for no one. This truth should leave us with an unsettled feeling, a feeling that will spur us forward toward the destiny and dreams that God has planned for our lives. Understand this: the enemy will gladly allow you to focus day in and day out on the wrong tasks and to cultivate the wrong relationships. We are of no real threat to the devil unless and until we set our hearts, minds, spirits, and bodies upon knowing and pleasing God each day.

Our priorities need to be reevaluated constantly. Nevertheless, some things should always be at the top. One, decide to give God your first, which is often your best. Do not wait to pray or read your Bible until after you have read the paper, responded to emails, or checked in on Facebook. Develop the discipline and practice of seeking God first and allowing Jesus' voice to be the One to set the tone for your day. Give God your first fruits in everything including your time, your talent, and your treasure.

Two, decide to invest in yourself spiritually to the same degree that you invest in your career, hobbies, and habits. Make it a practice to read a spiritual book each year, go on a spiritual retreat of revival and renewal, and take the time to measure your spiritual growth. If you are willing to invest in every other aspect of your life, you must be wise enough to keep building up the foundation upon which everything else stands: your spirit. Simply attending corporate worship one day a week is not enough to ensure that your life stays aligned with the ways of Christ. Remember, you cannot please a God whom you do not know, and you cannot know God without spending quality time in God's presence.

Three, decide to go after your God-given passion no matter what the cost. There is a dream that God birthed you to fulfill. There is a problem that should be solved, at least partially, through your life. Take the time to pay attention to the things, people, and circumstances that invoke passion and compassion from your life. These are the areas that you should prioritize. Yes, watching television is fun and traveling is very cool, but do not become satisfied with merely watching other people live their dreams. Do something each day to awaken the dreams that God has embedded in your heart. The freedom that you seek in life will not come from the outside; it will come when you allow Jesus to release His great power within. Once that power is unleashed, you will have what you need to continuously do the right thing. (Read Ephesians 3:14–21)

Week 14–Grief/Comfort
A Word to Sustain the Weary

Week 14—Grief/Comfort
A Word to Sustain the Weary

The Lord God has given me the tongue of a teacher, that I may know how to sustain the weary with a word.   (Isaiah 50:4a NRSV)

I n the times in which we live, there is no shortage of reasons to grieve. All around us, in our personal lives and in the media, there are stories of brokenness, pain, defeat, and death. An airplane carrying hundreds of passengers vanishes. A little girl is kidnapped. A fire devastates a neighborhood. Countries are on the brink of war. A man or woman is unjustly murdered in the streets. A pastor takes her own life. Our homes and schools are unsafe. The stories go on and on. As soon as we are *over* one tragedy we are thrown into another. Either directly or indirectly, we are often grappling with grief.

Grief is one of the most highly subjective and generally invasive concepts with which we must deal. Even when two people experience the same grief-causing incident, they will not grieve in the same way. Some people are criers, highly emotional and distraught when they grieve. Others are quiet, contemplative, and stoic. Some seem to be immobilized by grief, while others cast themselves into obsessive busyness as a distraction from their grief. Some of us are helped by being around people; others prefer to process and sort out our thoughts and feelings alone. In actuality, each of us finds ourselves experiencing most, if not all, of these descriptions at some point while we are grieving.

Indeed, the only real commonality about the way we grieve is that we grieve in stages. Grief is a process and it is different for each of us. You never know quite how you are going to feel at any given moment, especially during the early moments of grieving. Research has revealed that grief has the following stages: denial, anger, bargaining, depression, and acceptance (see grief.com for more information on these stages). While we can put our grief into stages, there is no guarantee that each of us will experience all five or that we will experience them in the same order. There is, in fact, an intentionality to grieving. We must allow ourselves the freedom and vulnerability to do it and we should offer this same freedom to our loved ones and friends. The universal truth is that no two people grieve in the same way or by the same schedule.

So, how do we grapple with grief? Well, we find good instruction and wisdom to help us in the word of God. The first thing we should understand when we are grieving is that God is available to us. Psalm 46:1 says, "God is our refuge and strength, a helper who is always found in times of trouble." (HCSB) When we are hurting, it is sometimes difficult to find friends and family members who understand and can help us. Nevertheless, God is always ready, willing, and able to help us if we are willing and able to let God into our grief process. In our times of distress, our cries and calls to the Lord will be heard and answered. (See Psalm 18:6)

Second, not only is God with us during our times of grief, pain, and difficulty, but also, God has just what we need. God is "the God of all comfort." (2 Corinthians 1:3) No matter what the circumstances are that have caused our grief, God always has the appropriate level of comfort for our hearts. Not all grief is the same. We grieve the physical death of loved ones and friends, and we also grieve over disappointments and setbacks. We grieve the loss of our dreams and the brokenness of our relationships. We never really "get over" some of these difficult life experiences.

Nevertheless, we can get through these times by allowing ourselves to grieve in a healthy way. This starts with simply acknowledging that we feel pain. Doing this invites Jesus Christ to give us the strength, peace, and even joy that we need to help us cope in life. For the truth is, as surely as there is brokenness, grief, and pain in life, there is also grace, strength, and comfort available from God.

This week, we will discuss how to grapple with grief with the intent of helping us to realize two things. First, God does not want our grieving to permanently disrupt and paralyze our living. Second, God comforts us during our times of grief so that we in turn can be a comfort to someone else. We are to be conduits of the very strength, grace, peace, and comfort which we ourselves have received. God will give you a word to sustain and comfort the weary, even when the weary one is you.

Blessed are those who mourn, for they will be comforted. (Matthew 5:4 NIV)

Questions to consider: How do you generally act when you are grieving? Do you suppress or outwardly express your grief? Are you able to recognize when you are *acting out* because you are grieving? Have you ever felt the comfort of God during a difficult time in life? How did it look? Feel?

Day 2—Let's Go a Little Deeper

When I suffer, this comforts me: Your promise gives me life. (Psalm 119:50 NCV)

Learning to appreciate grief can go a long way to help us process it. Yes, if we can be thankful for grief, we will be less likely to attach a stigma to it. Grief is not bad. It is not a sign of weakness. Rather it is an indication of strength when you can grieve your losses in life. When you can yet see God and recall God's promises during your affliction, you can know that your faith is mature.

Think about it this way: it is a sign of healthiness that we can feel pain. If you put your hand on the top of a hot stove and were unable to feel the heat, that would mean that your hand is not well. A healthy hand would send a message to the brain causing it to react and respond to the intense heat by drawing it back. The same idea is true when it comes to our psychology. If we do not respond and react to our spiritual, mental, and emotional pains, that is not a sense of strength; it is a sign that we are not well.

In fact, it may be an indication that we need help from a trained professional, if we continue to suppress and deny that we are hurting. The best life you can live is one completely devoted to Jesus Christ and God wants you to "prosper in every way and be in good health physically, just as you are spiritually." (3 John 2 HCSB) This simply means that God is concerned about every aspect of your life and wants you whole. God loves you completely; do not miss the opportunity to experience that love because you are not able to embrace it mind, body, soul, and spirit.

If you are willing to acknowledge and name your pain, you are on the right track. So, as you grapple with grief, keep a few things in mind:

Grieving takes time. Allow yourself (and others) time to grieve. Do not let anyone impose their timetable upon you. Time should be an element in each of our grief treatment plans. Depending upon the severity, your grief process may take less or more time. Nevertheless, if you can stay connected to the Lord throughout the process and willingly share your thoughts and feelings with God and others, you will sense God comforting you all along the way.

Grieving is a choice. You can get stuck in it or move forward through it.

Grieving takes work. Confront your sadness, express your pain, and even vent your anger; leaving these undone will only make you bitter, not better. Moreover, be willing to speak to a professional. There are many tools available to help us heal. Do not suffer alone or in silence. It is critical to not become isolated in our grief by buying into the enemy's lie that "no one will understand." It is true that: "Each heart knows its own bitterness, and no one else can share its joy." (Proverbs 14:10 NIV) However, we can receive strength from others while we are walking along our grief journey. Even though it is difficult to be vulnerable, we can gain so much through doing it.

Grieving does get better. Talk to anyone who has done the work of grieving and they must admit that it does get better. Take time to help someone else through their grief; you may be surprised by how much you help yourself in the process.

I would have lost heart, unless I had believed that I would see the goodness of the Lord in the land of the living. (Psalm 27:13 NKJV)

Day 3–Learning from Our Experiences

Recall and reflect or journal about a time when you had to grapple with grief. Did you avoid it or embrace it? What did you learn about God's comfort through that situation? Remember that God wants to comfort us, so that we can one day comfort someone else. This one thing is true: death, disappointments, pain, and problems happen to us all. Knowing this, we should be eager to not only be comforted in our times of need, but also to share comfort with those to whom we are connected and love. Comfort comes in many forms. It may be a hug, a prayer, a meal, or just being present. Comfort always involves listening, kindness, and genuine empathy. Be patient with yourself and others when it comes to grief. If you have not done a good job at this in the past, it is okay to start fresh today.

Meditate upon the following verses considering how you can posture yourself to receive and then give comfort. Is there anyone that you know who needs to be comforted today? Will you share it? Are you the person who needs comfort? Will you seek it?

Psalm 71:20–21: You, who have shown me great and severe troubles, shall revive me again, and bring me up again from the depths of the earth. You shall increase my greatness, and comfort me on every side. (NKJV)

Isaiah 66:13: As a mother comforts her child, so I will comfort you; you shall be comforted in Jerusalem. (NRSV)

Day 4–Biblical Character Reflection: Naomi (and Ruth)

"He oft finds present help, who does his grief impart." Edmund Spenser

Naomi's story is told in the book of Ruth. When we meet Naomi, she and her family have fled their home country of Bethlehem because of a famine. She ends up in Moab with her husband, two sons, and eventually two daughters-in-law. Over the course of time, however, Naomi's husband and sons died. She was left in a foreign land with only her two foreign daughters-in-law, Orpah and Ruth. Dejected and feeling empty, she headed back home. She called Orpah and Ruth to her and bid them ado.

Orpah left. Ruth remained. Ruth had also experienced the death of her husband, but instead of going back to her home and people, she stuck by her widowed mother-in-law. After Ruth and Naomi returned to Bethlehem, Naomi helps Ruth to meet and marry a new husband. In the process, they secure their future. Ruth ends up having a child that is in the lineage of Jesus Christ.

Naomi's story shows us that when we ourselves are hurting, we can still be a comfort and help to others. Moreover, in the process of helping another, we help ourselves. Naomi and Ruth had a lot in common. Even though Naomi wanted to be isolated and alone, she needed the love and companionship that Ruth offered to her. After receiving what she needed, Naomi in turn extended herself and gave to Ruth in ways that she did not even realize she needed. The moral is that we need each other. There are certainly times while we are grieving when we need to be alone to process and reflect upon our loss, whatever it is. Nevertheless, isolation and solitude can become harmful when not managed properly. It is imperative that we handle our grief with wisdom, being attentive to how we feel and what we need. It is also very important to realize that ". . . to whom much has been given, much will be required . . ." (Luke 12:48 NRSV) We find comfort, so that comfort can then be found in us.

Days 5-7—Making the Connection. Moving Forward.

All praise to God, the Father of our Lord Jesus Christ. God is our merciful Father and the source of all comfort. [God] comforts us in all our troubles so that we can comfort others. When they are troubled, we will be able to give them the same comfort God has given us. (2 Corinthians 1:3–4 NLT)

As we prepare to leave this week's topic, let us move forward with this understanding: God wants us to be healed and comforted from every loss that we have or will experience. It is not God's will for you to suffer indefinitely due to loss, brokenness, and disconnection. God can and will meet you at your point of need and carry you, by grace, to higher ground. God is the Source of all comfort; Jesus Christ is the Conduit of comfort into our lives. As we receive comfort from Christ, God expects and anticipates that we will become conduits of comfort for others.

Oftentimes when things happen to us, we automatically assume that whatever has happened is primarily about us. Fortunately, that logic is not always true. Some of the things we endure have little or nothing to do with us personally. Children must live (and sometimes suffer) with the mistakes of their parents. Players on the team must deal with the consequences of decisions made by their coaches and owners. We can seemingly do all the "right" things and still find ourselves as the recipient of unwarranted pain because hurt people eventually hurt people. Yes, every now and then, we must persevere through circumstances that are not necessarily our fault, but nonetheless become our burden. There is no easy answer for why this is so, but there is a perspective we can adopt to help us to overcome and endure.

We can choose to focus not so much upon the *why* of our circumstances and instead ask God to show us more clearly *who* God is and *what* we are to learn through our predicament. We can put our greatest effort into seeing and experiencing the presence of God with us in our difficult time, instead of merely lamenting the unfairness of our plight and begging God to make it all go away— quickly. Adopting this mentality requires that we see ourselves as conduits, not merely as containers.

Meaning this: we may not always know the reason for our hardships, but we can still make sense of them by choosing to pass along whatever good we learn (and experience) in the process. The fact of the matter is that the perspective we carry along our journey often determines the quality of the ride. Whether it is smooth or bumpy, swift or long, scenic or boring depends upon the eyes we take to it. The encouragement for us as we summarize this week's study is to choose to see the heart and hand of God in all things. God's heart is always loving and God's hand is always powerful and strong. Decide that no matter what you may experience in life, be it triumph or tragedy, you will know God better through it all. Determine that as you know better, you will trust more.

Not everything is about punishment, and if we look closely enough we can see that in everything there is an opportunity to witness God's fulfilled promises. How could we ever grasp the blessing of being comforted, if we did not first know the pain of grief? Which of us could ever be called a child of God, if we are not first confronted with violence and yet choose to make peace? (See Matthew 5:4, 9)

No, God does not make us suffer to prove some point that may forever remain elusive. But yes, what Christ said is true: "In this world you will have trouble" and suffering because evil is real and the evil one is relentlessly committed to your destruction. (John 16:33; 10:10) How we deal with suffering will most certainly determine the quality (and sometimes the quantity) of our days. No matter our circumstance, God has promised through the person and power of Jesus Christ to shower us with comfort, strength, peace, wisdom, and grace. What if we decided to share those very same things with the hurting, dying, and fragile people who surround us each day? We can be conduits of comfort. By God's help and in Christ's strength, we can extend grace in subtle and profound ways.

We can look all around us, near us and even within us to see that there is a need for kindness, grace, and comfort. As a society, we seem to be so moved by the pain of certain people—those who are prominent, beautiful, and fair. While the despair and hardships of those who are unknown, poor, and dark very often go unnoticed. But, here's the truth: there is no drought of love, compassion, tears, or even prayer in our world. Our issue is and always has been how those and other resources are distributed. Nevertheless, we cannot give what we do not have, or what we do not know that we possess. That is why we must decide to let God give us comfort. We must open our hearts and minds to the idea of finally letting some tensions die, some wounds heal, and some pains subside. It will not be easy to start a new pattern. In fact, getting healthy will feel harder than the initial injury at some points along the journey. But, God is with you, and on the other side of the storm is a peaceful shore.

Once you reach that place, and even while you are still journeying there, point others toward the way. Do not set yourself up as the standard, for everyone's course must be unique. But, point others to the God, the Savior, the Friend, the Confidant, who held you during your midnight. Point others to the One who yet wipes away your tears. Release some of what you have already received from the hand of God; then there will be enough to go around.

Believe that you can be a conduit carrying good to the people and the places that need it most, even if they are right down the street, in the next office, or perhaps sitting just across the table from you. You do have a word that will help sustain the weary. It is the same word that was spoken to you during your time of weariness and despair:

Come to Me, all of you who are weary and burdened, and I will give you rest. All of you, take up My yoke and learn from Me, because I am gentle and humble in heart, and you will find rest for yourselves. For My yoke is easy and My burden is light. (Matthew 11:28–30 HCSB)

Week 15–Joy
This Joy That I Have!

Week 15–Joy
This Joy That I Have!

And the angel said unto them, Fear not: for, behold, I bring you good tidings of great joy, which shall be to all people.   (Luke 2:10 KJV)

Do you have joy? Your immediate answer is most likely, "Yes, of course!" Here's the thing: joy is not best expressed through words, but rather it is best expressed through how we live our lives. A lifestyle of joy comes only from a true relationship with Jesus Christ. In fact, joy itself is a by-product of our salvation. When we open our lives to a loving, growing, dynamic relationship with God by believing in Jesus, we get joy. That's good news! The issue, however, is not getting joy. The complicated part is keeping our joy through all the twists and turns, ups and downs, good and bad times of life.

For, even though joy is available, it does not mean it will be present in our lives. We must receive it; we must grab it; and we must hold on to it. We do this by allowing the Holy Spirit to have free rein in our lives so that the fruit of joy can be cultivated within us. Understand that joy is not created by human or tangible means. Joy has one source —the Spirit of the Living God. One reason that it can be difficult to maintain joy is because we may not fully understand it. Joy is not happiness. Happiness is based upon the external. It is connected to what is going on outside of us and around us. Happiness is based upon happenings. When our happenings are good, we have happiness. Happiness is not bad; it is a lovely gift of God. Nevertheless, happiness pales in comparison to joy.

Joy is an inside job. Joy is based upon a deep and abiding connection to God through Jesus Christ. Joy is an internal reality that allows us to overcome and hover over any external happenings. Having and living in joy does not mean that you are not able to acknowledge sadness and disappointment. Having joy simply means that the presence of sadness and disappointment does not cause you to lose sight of the goodness and grace that are also there.

This week we will take a closer look at getting, maintaining, and living with joy. Joy is available to you in abundance. How much joy can you stand?

Questions to consider: What is your definition of joy? How do you currently seek to cultivate joy in your life? Are you joyful or simply happy? How do you handle uncertain times? Do you maintain your joy or do you tend to become disgruntled?

Day 2–Let's Go a Little Deeper

Dear brothers and sisters, when troubles of any kind come your way, consider it an opportunity for great joy. For you know that when your faith is tested, your endurance has a chance to grow. So let it grow, for when your endurance is fully developed, you will be perfect and complete, needing nothing. (James 1:2–4 NLT)

Believe it or not, it is a decision to be joyful. When we choose joy, we open our hearts and lives to many other blessings. James tells us in the passage above that it is our response and reaction to the various trials, temptations, and dilemmas of life, which help to determine how much we grow. Do you want to grow and mature in Christ? If so, choose joy.

Choosing joy is something that we must do continuously. As life unfolds, we will be presented with opportunities that will allow us to choose to be joyful. That is what James shares with us through the quoted passage. It is about our perspective. Do you see the storms and challenges of life as an opportunity to learn, to trust, and to obey the word of God? Or, do you take the hard things that happen to you as a personal affront? There are ways which God can strengthen us in and through our trials, which will not happen any other way. We are open and alert during times of difficulty. Moreover, in the hard times, we are often more willing to listen to God's voice because we are keenly aware of our inadequacies.

God does not necessarily cause or make us go through trials and painful circumstances. Nevertheless, trials, hardships, and challenges are a part of living in a fallen, sin-ridden world. (See John 16:33) Evil persists and therefore, indignities, negativity, and problems will exist until Christ returns. Even so, we can always gain from even the toughest of circumstances, if we have the right perspective. The hardest person for you to truly see sometimes is you. One benefit of remaining alert, open, and teachable in every season of life is that you can stay connected to yourself; how you handle the trials of life gives you a glimpse into what is inside of your heart and mind. It reveals the quality of your faith.

Do you seem to be faced with the same issue repeatedly? Have you noticed that you are annoyed, frustrated, or plagued by the same personality type on your job or in your family? Maybe God is trying to tell you something. Perhaps, it is time for you to choose a different reaction to those people and situations. We have more power and control in our lives than we often realize. What happens to us is nothing compared to what God has already done for us and what Jesus still desires to do in us and through us; but the choice is ours. Today, and every day, I choose joy! What about you?

Rejoice in the Lord always. I will say it again: Rejoice! (Philippians 4:4 HCSB)

Day 3—Learning from Our Experiences

Recall and reflect or journal about a time when you made the deliberate choice to be joyful during a challenging circumstance. How did choosing joy impact how you maneuvered through that time? Has there ever been a time when you did not choose joy, but looking back now, you wish you had? Do you think that you would have come through that circumstance better or more quickly if you had made the choice to be joyful? What often hinders you from choosing joy?

Meditate upon the following verses considering how to become more aware of God's abiding presence. How does being with God fill your life with joy? Make a list of the ways that joy can come into (and flow out of) your life. What can you do today to make sure that joy is more prominent in your life? What is blocking the flow of joy through your life that you can stop doing?

Psalm 16:11: You will teach me how to live a holy life. Being with you will fill me with joy; at your right hand, I will find pleasure forever. (NCV)

Habakkuk 3:18: . . . I will rejoice in the LORD, I will be joyful in God my Savior. (NIV)

Day 4–Biblical Character Reflection: Nehemiah

*And Nehemiah, who was the governor, and Ezra the priest and scribe, and the Levites who taught the people said to all the people, "This day is holy to the Lord your God; do not mourn or weep." For all the people wept when they heard the words of the law. Then he said to them, "Go your way, eat the fat and drink sweet wine and send portions of them to those for whom nothing is prepared, for this day is holy to our Lord; and do not be grieved, **for the joy of the LORD is your strength**."* (Nehemiah 8:9–10 NRSV, emphasis added)

Nehemiah was a leader of Judah who, after he learned of its desolation, returned to the holy city of Jerusalem to lead the rebuilding effort. His story can be read in the book of Nehemiah. Nehemiah lived in Persia after the time of exile and served as the cupbearer to King Artaxerxes (Nehemiah 1 and 2). When Nehemiah first learned of the ruined state of the holy city, he sat down and wept for many days. His heavy and sad countenance eventually got the attention of the king. Once the king learned what was troubling Nehemiah, he gave him permission to go back to Jerusalem to survey the condition of the walls and gates. Moreover, the king gave Nehemiah the resources he would need to rebuild. It is important to recognize those to whom you are connected in every season of your life. God often gives us what we need through those who are right beside us. And, God often wants us to be a blessing to those who are close to us, both physically and relationally.

It took Nehemiah and the team he assembled about six months to rebuild the wall after fighting through much opposition. After the walls and gates had been rebuilt, many of the exiles returned to Jerusalem. It was then that Ezra, the priest, called for the Book of the Law. Ezra read the book out loud to the people. Upon hearing all that was required in the law and realizing how they had failed to uphold the word and standard of God, the people cried. They were convicted, saddened, stressed, and disappointed in themselves and in their ancestors. It was at this point that Nehemiah steps up to give them some wise albeit surprising advice: he told them to rejoice.

Nehemiah told the people that it was the joy of the Lord that would be their strength. Nehemiah was not saying that they should ignore the law or the conviction they felt, knowing that their behavior had fallen short of God's standards. No, he was essentially saying, even though they felt sad and convicted, they could still rejoice because they now knew the truth and had an opportunity to get it right.

They could rejoice because the God who gave the law and the promises attached thereto is still faithful, just, and true. Joy comes through our faith—believing that God is who God says God is. Joy can coexist with sadness and unhappiness because the source of joy is different from those other two. If we attempt to anchor our joy in anything other than our faith in Jesus Christ, it will not withstand the tests and trials of life. However, if we can remain focused upon God even through our sorrow, we can have peace in our hearts and joy inside our tears.

We, like the residents of Jerusalem in Nehemiah's day, must understand that we gain strength, power, insight, and motivation to keep running our race when we maintain our joy throughout every season of life. Our joy says that we believe God. Our joy says that we trust God. Our joy says, things may be bad, but I am still victorious—through Christ.

What captures your attention about Nehemiah and how he handled a challenging season in his life? How can you stand up in the face of opposition?

Days 5-7–Making the Connection. Moving Forward.

I have told you these things, that My joy and delight may be in you, and that your joy and gladness may be of full measure and complete and overflowing. (John 15:11 AMP)

To summarize all that we have studied this week about joy consider this: joy is always appropriate. We can and should have joy in every situation and throughout every season of our lives. We know that this is true because all throughout the Bible the Christian discipline of joy is mentioned and extolled. From Nehemiah in the Old Testament to Jesus in the New Testament, we see that learning the discipline of joy is critical to us living God-honoring lives. Moreover, we should understand that it is expected that our joy will be full, complete, and overflowing because of our relationship with Christ.

Joy is an internal disposition that comes from knowing God and loving Jesus. Joy comes from having a faith that says, no matter what my eyes may see and my heart may feel, I know that all things are yet working together for my good. (See Romans 8:28) Joy is about trusting who God is and believing in the promises that only God can and will fulfill in our lives. Joy is our right as born-anew believers in Jesus Christ. Joy is our reinforcement and our reasonable response to God. Therefore, the parting word for you this week is simply this: take joy with you! Wherever this life takes you, whatever terrain you must traverse, be sure to take joy along with you on the journey.

How, you ask? The answer is by following the example of Jesus Christ. Perhaps one of the best stories to show the appropriateness of joy in all circumstances is the story of Palm Sunday, leading into Christ's week of passion and suffering, found in Luke 19.

Jesus began His journey toward His crucifixion upon Golgotha's Hill with rejoicing and celebration. At first glance, it may seem a little strange that Jesus would create the scenario, putting Himself and others in the position of being filled with joy, just days before He would be wrongfully accused, unjustly convicted, and killed. But, for our sakes, it is a good thing that Jesus did this because He shows us how to handle life's great contradictions, stresses, and pains with dignity and joy.

As we leave our study of joy this week, consider these three ways, drawn from Luke 19: 28–40, that you can take joy with you wherever you may be required to go.

Follow What Jesus Says (verses 30–35): Our journey in life will be helped if we can keep this one thing in mind: Jesus already knows. So, when life starts to happen and difficulties begin to unfold, make it a point not to deviate from the words and instruction of Jesus. What Jesus has said will come to pass. We can maintain our joy by simply maintaining our obedience through every season and situation of life.

In our passage, Jesus gave instructions to the disciples and they followed those directives and found everything just as Jesus said it would be. Oftentimes along our journey, we either forget or simply neglect Christ's instructions. Jesus' words contain life guidance, help, healing, and wisdom. We must discipline ourselves to remain faithful and obedient to the words of Christ in both the simple and in the complex circumstances of our lives. If we will continue to have joy, we must first choose to trust and obey God's Word.

Focus on What You Have Seen (verses 37–38): Staying focused and locked in on what Jesus has already done is equally important to maintaining our joy as remembering what Jesus has said. Our text in Luke 19:37 says, "The whole crowd of disciples began joyfully to praise God in loud voices for all the miracles they had seen." (NIV) Those in the crowd had varying moods for sure, but some of them were there giving thanks and praise to Jesus because of the miracles that they had seen. They believed that if they had seen Jesus do it before, there was a chance that they could see it again. They were both hopeful and joyful. We must be the same. You have an experience with God. Focus on what you already know to be true, even while you are waiting for what you are hoping, praying, and trusting to be manifested by God.

. . . The just shall live by faith. (Romans 1:17b NKJV)

Remember, the **Future Is Secure** (verses 39–40): Ultimately, we can remain joyful throughout every season and situation of life because we know that in Jesus our future is secure. Even as Jesus was preparing to endure the hardest moments of His life, He did not lose sight of who He was. Jesus knew His purpose and Jesus could allow for celebration just days before His crucifixion because He knew that the future was secure. This is our hope as well. Jesus says to the Pharisees who rebuked Him and told Him to quiet down His followers, that even if they were to be quiet, the rocks would cry out. This is essentially what the psalmist declares:

> The heavens tell the glory of God, and the skies announce what [God's] hands have made. Day after day they tell the story; night after night they tell it again. They have no speech or words; they have no voice to be heard. But their message goes out through all the world; their words go everywhere on earth. (Psalm 19:1–4a NCV)

When life gets hard, remember that you know the end of the story. Jesus wins, and since we are on the Lord's side, we win as well. We are yet more than conquerors through God who loves us. (See Romans 8:37) If you have Jesus, your future is secure. This knowledge should bring you joy.

Let us fix our eyes on Jesus, the author and perfecter of our faith, who for the joy set before him endured the cross, scorning its shame, and sat down at the right hand of the throne of God. (Hebrews 12:2 NIV)

Week 16—Yielding to God's Will
Lead Me, Guide Me, along the Way

Week 16–Yielding to God's Will
Lead Me, Guide Me, along the Way

The LORD directs the steps of the godly. He delights in every detail of their lives. (Psalm 37:23 NLT)

There are seasons and moments in life when knowing what to do next can be a conundrum. Sometimes this is true because we have too many options. At other times, it is because we feel as if we have too few. Either way, the answer is not as easy to discern as we would like. Alternatively, the issue may not be that we do not know which way to go, but rather that we do not want to do what is right or best.

While we should cultivate the spiritual practice of obedience in our lives, sometimes disobeying the nagging voice of God just seems easier and better in the moment. We know we should tell the truth, but the truth can be long and complicated. Lies are sometimes quick and easy. We know that we should work, or read, or save, but "adulting" all day every day can be nerve racking. In fact, often the most difficult aspect of doing the will of God is first yielding our own wills and proclaiming to God, like Jesus did, "Not what I will, but what You will." (Mark 14:36 HCSB)

It goes without saying that we hear God's voice better when we are open to whatever it is that God wants to say. But, it is okay to be honest about the fact that sometimes we do not want, nor feel like we need, God's guidance and direction. Nevertheless, after you are honest, you should face this simple truth: there is no freedom, no solace, no enduring peace, outside of the purpose and will of God for your life. No matter where you are or what you are currently experiencing, when the dust settles, and the noise subsides, this truth becomes almost audible. We hasten our own maturity when we embrace this fact and live each day seeking to align ourselves with the purpose of God, which is greater and better than anything we could ever imagine.

This week, we will study the concept of yielding to God's will. Our goal is to empower and encourage you to stay attentive to God's voice and obedient to God's guidance all along life's journey. Here are a few foundational principles which we must embrace to make the process of yielding more manageable. Starting today, make these a part of your daily confessions; we will delve into each of these, later in the week.

God has a plan for my life and it is beautiful.

God wants me to know God's plans for my life.

God's timing is impeccable.

Trust in the LORD with all your heart, and **lean not** *on your own understanding; in all your ways acknowledge Him, and He* **shall direct** *your paths.* (Proverbs 3:5–6 NKJV, emphasis added)

Questions to consider: In general, which is harder for you: hearing from the Lord, or obediently walking out what you have heard? Do you know God's purpose for your life? If so, can you articulate it, to yourself or to someone that you trust today? What makes it hard for you to trust God's plan for your life?

Day 2–Let's Go a Little Deeper

Order my steps in Thy word: and let not any iniquity have dominion over me. (Psalm 119:133 KJV)

The verse quoted above is a prayer that details four elements that we need to know and follow in order to do the will of God for our lives. Let us break it down.

Order. Order and intention are two key aspects of God's methodology in dealing with humanity. Down through time and history, we have seen numerous examples of how God moves. God takes calculated and deliberate steps. Jesus is conscientious, strategic, and wise. If you will stay yielded to God's will, you must abandon yourself to God's process of working. You must keep trusting. First, trust that God has a process. And second, trust that the process is working.

Yes, there will be moments when we are unsure about what God is doing. God's process may not seem logical per human standards, but God knows how to get us where we need to be, when we need to be there. And, God also knows how to surround us with the right people. God is trustworthy and does everything well. God has a plan and that plan is ordered. Trust that God's plans always work together for your good. (See Romans 8:28)

Steps. Jesus rarely gives us our directions in one sitting. Sure, it *can* happen that way. There may be times when God will roll out an entire plan and show us the broad steps in toto. It is more common, however, that God will show us the plan one step at a time. Even when God gives us a clear vision of our future, there are often intricacies, layers, and phases, which will take time for us to grasp fully. Jesus knows that we can only handle so much information at a time. Therefore, God reveals details to us on a need-to-know basis. Meaning, God often reveals the next step to us when we need (not when we want) to know it. This is an incredibly gracious way for God to work because it requires that we trust, watch, and wait. The process is made easier when we remember that wherever we are going is ultimately going to be good. (See again Romans 8:28)

The Word. God always moves in accordance with the Word. Be clear; God is not limited by anything or anyone, including the Bible. Nevertheless, it is not in God's nature or character to contradict the Word of God. We can trust God's Word to be a lamp and a light to our feet and pathway. (See Psalm 119:105) And, we can trust God to act consistently with what we see revealed about God in the Bible.

The word shows us how God has interacted and engaged with women and men since the dawning of creation. Thus, the biblical record is a great barometer for the situations and circumstances of our lives. We can draw wisdom, grace, peace, strength, hope, direction, and power from reading and rereading the Bible stories. Expect the Lord to lead you. Look for guidance in the Word.

Prayer. It would be misleading to say that all we need to do is read the Bible repeatedly to find direction. Prayer is integral to our ability to hear clearly from God. When we settle our hearts, minds, and spirits through prayer, we allow the Holy Spirit to interpret the words of the Bible and the situations of our lives. God's voice sounds unique and different to each of us. Through the dialogue of prayer, we gain revelation that cannot be gained through any other means. And, what God gives us through our times of prayer will sustain us when everything else seems to fail. Prayer is not simply talking to Jesus, but prayer is communing with God. Take your prayer life up in quality and quantity and everything else in your life will shift accordingly.

The LORD says, I will guide you along the best pathway for your life. I will advise you and watch over you. (Psalm 32:8 NLT)

Day 3–Learning from Our Experiences

Earlier in the week, we referenced three fundamental principles which we need to embrace so that we can yield to God's purpose and will for our lives. Today we will look more closely at those principles.

God has a plan and it is beautiful. Here is what the Bible declares in 1 Corinthians 2:9: ". . . no eye has seen, no ear has heard, and no mind has imagined the things that God has prepared for those who love [God]." (GW) God is in the business of preparing good things for God's children. This was true about the plan God developed to save humanity, and it is true about the plans that God has for every aspect of your life. God is always working behind, in front of, and in the scenes of our lives to bring God's perfect plans to pass.

Our job? Trust, obey, follow, watch, listen, learn, yield; and repeat. We can trust that the will of God for our lives is perfectly beautiful. It may not be a straight line. It may not always make you happy. Nevertheless, what God is developing in you as you come in line with God's perfect and beautiful plan will not disappoint you. Let this truth sink deeply into your heart.

Yet, O LORD, you are our Father; we are the clay, and you are our potter; we are all the work of your hand. (Isaiah 64:8 NRSV)

God wants me to know God's plan for my life. One of the incorrect thoughts that many people have about the will of God for their life is that they must search and work to *figure it out.* This is not the idea that we see revealed through scripture, however. God delights to tell us the plans for our lives. Now, as mentioned yesterday, we may not get all the facts that we want when we want them, but we will get the direction that we need. The truth is that it would not serve God or you for God to hide the ball or make your purpose a deep mystery. God wants you to know the truth, so that you can be set free to live it out each day.

Here is what the Bible says in 1 Corinthians 2:10: "But God **has shown us** these things through the Spirit. The Spirit searches out all things, even the deep secrets of God." (NCV, emphasis added) Even though God has plans for our lives that we could never imagine or understand on our own, by the Holy Spirit, God shows these things to us. The will of God for your life is not a mystery that needs to be solved. It is an intricate plan, which will be revealed to you as you develop an abiding and trusting relationship with Jesus Christ.

Some things are hidden. They belong to the LORD our God. But the things that have been revealed in these teachings belong to us and to our children forever. We must obey every word of these teachings. (Deuteronomy 29:29 GW)

God's timing is impeccable. Without question, one of the most difficult aspects of yielding to and trusting the will of God is the fact that at times it seems to take soooo looonnnggg. Waiting when you have all the details is hard. Waiting when you cannot see the full picture is grueling. Nevertheless, the truth is that God's timing is perfect. God is never late. God never wastes time. As we trust God's plan and obey God's instructions for our lives, everything (people and experiences) that is meant for us will be ours at just the right moment.

What we must remember is that we only know and see a small part of the bigger plan. God shows us what we need and what we can handle. We do not have all the inside knowledge and understanding that Jesus has. So, when it seems like the process is taking too long, it may be that we (or the circumstance) are not quite ready. As you wait, keep telling yourself that God is too intentional, too loving, too deliberate, and too kind to allow you to miss God's perfect plan.

As Jesus said, "The Father is the only One who has the authority to decide dates and times. These things are not for you to know." (Acts 1:7 NCV) But, what we do know is that when it all comes together, and the perfect plan unfolds, it will be good; and we will be amazed.

Recall and reflect or journal about a time when one or more of these principles proved to be true in your life. Describe how you felt when you saw that God's plan was coming together. Meditate upon the following verses. Ask God to reveal to you any areas of sin or disobedience in your life. Ask God to show you where you may be resisting God's will. Determine to yield.

Psalm 119:10–11: I seek you with all my heart; do not let me stray from your commands. I have hidden your word in my heart that I might not sin against you. (NIV)

Day 4–Biblical Character Reflection: Jesus in the Garden of Gethsemane

Jesus is our perfect example for how to live a life fully surrendered to God. During His time on earth, Jesus showed us how to marry the spiritual, physical, emotional, and mental aspects of our lives, to ensure that God always gets the glory. Even though Jesus was fully God, He was also fully human and that means that He had a free will just like we do. Jesus could have chosen not to fulfill His destiny. He could have decided that He did not want to pay the high cost to save humanity from eternal destruction and separation from God. Nevertheless, by the power of the Holy Spirit, Jesus freely yielded His will to do God's perfect will for His life. Jesus erected no barriers or limitations to the Holy Spirit working in His life. Jesus allowed the Holy Spirit complete access to every area of His life, nothing was off-limits. We can live this same way.

Free will has always been a strange concept to many. At first thought, it seems like it would be better for God to simply *force* us to do God's will for our lives. After all, God knows that what God has planned is what is best for us. But, when we think about it deeper, we can rest assured that God did not make a mistake by giving humanity free will and choice. For there is power in deciding to do something; and when you are invested in the process, it generally makes you more committed to the outcome.

For some reason when something is forced, it is less meaningful, less authentic, and we are generally less committed to it. For you see, while God's way is best *for* us and will prove to bring the best *out* of us, God does not simply shove it down our throats. No, God wants you to want what is best. God wants you to want a relationship; God wants you to freely choose to make cultivating a growing, dynamic relationship with Jesus Christ a priority. God wants you to want the divine will that has been created for your life. God knows that only when you choose, will you stay committed to it for the long haul. Commitment is a critical component to seeing the manifestation of all that God has designed for your life. This was true for Jesus and it is no less true for you.

In Mark 14, in the Garden of Gethsemane, Jesus found Himself on the brink of His destiny. (See vs. 32–42) Jesus had to make a choice to either acquiesce to his feelings or submit His will to God's will. Thankfully, He chose the latter and at that moment the course of history changed forever. Here are three points that we can glean from how Jesus handled the biggest night in His life.

Secure Your Support (verses 33–34): Jesus models for us the importance of having a support system as we yield to God's will for our lives. Those who know us, love us, and encourage us become invaluable along the journey toward our destiny. At the very moment when you would quit, a friend, mentor, or confidant can give you just the nudge you need to make it across the finish line. Today, consider who you want (and need) with you as you face the certain and uncertain seasons of life. You will need some support along the way. Choose wisely.

Persist in Prayer (verses 35–36; 39): Even though we know what a powerful tool prayer is, sometimes we neglect to use it as much as we should. Instead of staying in prayer about life until we have the answer or the peace we need, we often give up too quickly. We can incorrectly assume that if we persist in prayer, it somehow means that we lack faith. The opposite is true, however. We gain faith to do that which we are called to do when we are willing to persist with God in prayer.

Look at Jesus. Our text indicates that He prays not once, not twice, but three times on this most crucial night. Jesus did not merely utter nice words, but rather He got alone and threw Himself before God in prayer. His prayers are nearly identical each time, proving the fact that yielding to the will of God is not an overnight or instantaneous occurrence. But rather, it is a process that takes time, energy, and commitment. Prayer is the type of thing that the more you do it, the more strength you gain to keep doing it. God can give us the right spirit and attitude when we pray. God can remind us of God's truths when we linger in prayer. We can also be reminded of God's sovereignty and sufficiency when we pray with an open heart. Most of all we can be convinced of God's presence and assured of God's love. Do not simply pray about God's will for your life; persist in prayer. Do not let go until you get your blessing.

Determine to Do It (verse 42): After Jesus prayed to God three times for clarity and strength to do God's will, the only thing left was for Him to do it. And, He got up and went straight to it. We do not find Jesus making excuses, blaming the shortcomings of His friends, negotiating or strategizing about how to flee, or in any way seeking to delay the inevitable. Jesus simply determined that He would do God's will and He did it. He yielded His very life for our salvation.

Understand this: your praying, seeking, fasting, coming to church, giving your tithe, and walking by faith, must culminate in you actually doing the will of God. There is no way around it. In fact, many of us have done everything else except this critical step. We know the direction in which we should be moving and yet we are standing still. It may be because of fear of failure (or success) or because we are focused on the external instead of the eternal God who is calling us. Whatever the reason for your stagnation, one thing is true. There is an aspect of God's will that you are simply not going to see until you get up and start doing it. The longer you sit on the sidelines waiting to see the whole picture, the more miserable you will become. Just do it. Like God was with Jesus, God is with you.

Days 5-7—Making the Connection. Moving Forward.

For I know the plans I have for you, says the Lord. They are plans for good and not for disaster, to give you a future and a hope. (Jeremiah 29:11 NLT)

This week we have sought to convince you that the ultimate peace, power, and joy which you are seeking in life can be found only by yielding your will to the will of God. The answers to the questions you have been posing to God about your purpose and calling may be more properly directed inward, as you ask yourself, "Have I honestly said to God, 'Thy will be done'?" Whether we know it or not, doing the will of God for our lives is very simple. It boils down to one word: obedience. The process of being obedient is not simple, however, it will take you a lifetime to perfect. Nevertheless, the benefits of learning to walk in obedience to the voice and call of Jesus will far outweigh the challenges that are sure to come along the way.

We have focused on our need to stay open, attentive, and yielded to God's voice and God's plan for our lives. To do this, we must remember that all of God's plans are good and much better than what we could come up with on our own. God's purpose and destiny will require much more of you than you want to give, and it will stretch you in ways that you do not want to go. Yet, as you relax and release your will to God's will, you will find that God's plan is perfect and perfectly fit for you.

In all honesty, obedience is not hard unless we try to separate it from love. Jesus says it this way: "Those who accept my commandments and obey them are the ones who love me." (John 14:21a NLT) In Jesus' mind, there is no love without obedience. Many times, when we see the word "commands" we automatically think of the Ten Commandments or some explicit rule or regulation. And, while this is correct, the reality is that even that still small voice in your heart, that nudge to go left, or that press to make a phone call or share a word—are all commands that need to be obeyed. The practice and pattern of your life must be that you harken to the voice of God no matter how subtle or boisterous it may be. Jesus is always speaking. Jesus is always guiding us and directing our steps. The question is: are we alert and attentive to His voice and do we have an attitude of obedience toward what is being shared?

The good news is that we do not have to walk out obedience in our own power. The Holy Spirit is there to help us each step of the way. The Spirit will empower us to go well beyond our human limitations. We only need to be willing to receive the power that God's Spirit offers to us.

Moreover, remember that your obedience and willingness to trust, yield, and obey God's voice will always be rewarded. Jesus goes on to say: "And because they love me, my Father will love them. And I will love them and reveal myself to each of them."

(John 14:21b NLT) When we, by our obedience, show our love to Jesus, Jesus shows His love right back to us. Our reward for following obediently is that Jesus reveals more and more of who He is to us each day. The more we learn to recognize Him, the easier it is to follow. The more we follow, the deeper the revelation we will receive and the cycle will continue from one level of faith to the next. It all starts with obedience—the highest act of adoration and love that we can show to the Lord.

As the Father has loved me, so have I loved you. Now remain in my love. If you obey my commands, you will remain in my love, just as I have obeyed my Father's commands and remain in His love. (John 15:9–10 NIV)

Week 17–Expectations
Looking for a Miracle?!

Week 17–Expectations
Looking for a Miracle?!

But sheer awe swept over them and they kept saying to each other,
Whoever can He be? - even the wind and the waves do what He tells
them! (Mark 4:41 Phillips NT)

What is your definition of a miracle? Is it something that is abnormal, out of the ordinary, or simply inexplicable? Oftentimes, we consider a miracle to be something that we cannot or do not see often. We consider miracles to be things like unexplained healings, unexpected movements in nature, and even reversals of fortune. What if we expanded this definition? What would our lives and world look like if we began to understand that miracles are all around us every day—in the things that we consider common? The fact is: we most often get exactly what we expect and plan to receive. There are, of course, exceptions to this rule, but it is nonetheless true. So, are you looking for a miracle?

It is correct to call those things which are seemingly contrary to nature a miracle. That is what happened in Mark 4:41. The disciples had just witnessed Jesus speak to the wind and the waves and they both obeyed His command. They were in awe. Rightfully so! It is also correct to consider our everyday living, moving, and being as a miracle. This is not a way to dumb down the meaning of miracles, but rather a way to expand our appreciation for all that Jesus Christ is and all that Christ does and desires to do.

If we can train our eyes and minds to see that God is always working, we can deepen our faith and strengthen our resolve. Deeper faith will allow us to experience more of God. The more of

God that we get, the more of God we will want. God is unlimited in wisdom, strength, and power. By faith in Jesus, we have access to a limitless God, who is able and willing to perform miracles in us, for us, and through us.

Now certainly, we will still experience sin, sickness, death, disease, and violence in this world. This is what Jesus referred to in John 16 when He said, ". . . In this world you will have trouble. But take heart! I have overcome the world." (verse 33 NIV) One way that we can *take heart* is to learn to better appreciate the moments of holiness, health, life, and peace, which surround us. Things are bad, but they are not all bad. People are difficult, and yet people are kind as well. Shifting our focus away from the hardness and toward the good will radically impact our lives and cause our love for God to grow.

For example, someone may be dealing with an illness, and yet to be able to get out of the bed without pain shooting through their legs is a miracle. Someone else may be estranged from family or friends; nevertheless, receiving an unexpected phone call, or seeing the face of a loved one after years of separation is indeed a miracle. Miracles are everywhere all the time. Miracles help to break up the stress, pressure, and turmoil that often characterize our lives and give us hope. Miracles remind us that another reality is possible. Miracles reveal the depth of God's character and convince us that God is ever-willing to bless us. **God is a God of miracles!** Miracles are easy to God. God does not simply perform a miracle every now and then. Far from that, God is always doing the miraculous. The question is, can you see it?

This week we will seek to expand our minds, hearts, eyes, and ears about miracles so that we can look for and see them more clearly. The way to do this is not by looking for miracles at all. The trick is to get in a better position to see the God who is orchestrating the miraculous in us and around us each day. For, if we can become more familiar with the ways and working of the Divine, we—like the disciples in Jesus' day—will sit, stand, and live in awe of our Lord.

When the people saw Him do this miraculous sign, they exclaimed, 'Surely, He is the Prophet we have been expecting!' (John 6:14 NLT)

Questions to consider: What is your definition of a miracle? Have you ever experienced a miracle? What was it? How did it make you feel? What did experiencing that miracle show you about Jesus?

Day 2—Let's Go a Little Deeper

May your kingdom come and what you want be done, here on earth as it is in heaven. (Matthew 6:10 NCV)

For our purposes this week, we should have a working definition of miracles. Let us agree that miracles are simply the manifestation of heaven on earth. In the model or Lord's Prayer found in Matthew, quoted above, Jesus instructs the disciples to ask that God's will be done on earth as it is in heaven. God's perfect plan always happens in heaven. In heaven, there are not barriers, obstructions, or obstacles to the will of God. The same is not true here on earth. On earth, we must pray, act, agitate, hope, and decide that the will of God will be done. The fact that God has a perfect will for what happens on earth does not mean that it will automatically happen. We must want and make room for God's will to be done. Thus, whenever we see the desire of God's heart manifested here on earth, we are looking at a miracle.

So, what does God desire? God wants humanity to walk together in peace, unity, and strength. (See Psalm 133) God wants us to love one another the same way that Jesus has loved us. (See John 15:12) God wants everyone to repent and receive everlasting life. (See 2 Peter 3:9) God wants us to be new, to be reconciled to God, so that we can be reconciled to one another. God wants relationships restored, forgiveness extended and accepted, and chasms overcome. (See 2 Corinthians 5:18–20)

Ultimately, God wants us to live life like Jesus did while He was on earth. Jesus showed us how to live by faith and through the power of the Holy Spirit. Jesus showed us that when the Holy Spirit has unfettered access to our lives, the will of God can be done in the earth realm to the same degree and effectiveness as it happens in heaven. In other words, we can experience the miraculous.

The thing is, we must be looking for and expecting God to bring us into these miracles. If we are not alert and sober, we may miss them. In fact, we are to not only look for miracles, but also, we should avail ourselves to God's power and Spirit, as Jesus did, so that we can be miracle workers.

God's perfect will does not always find space on earth because there is evil and an enemy who is also working. The devil works to pervert, undo, interrupt, confuse, and deter the perfect will of God on earth. God expelled satan from heaven for this very reason. Satan was an angel who was gifted and beautiful, yet he was not satisfied with that. He was not content pointing to God and giving God glory through his existence. He wanted the glory, attention, and honor that rightfully belongs only to God, for himself. So, satan had to leave heaven. (Read Isaiah 14:15 and Ezekiel 28:16–17)

Now, satan is trying the same thing on earth that he tried in heaven. Satan wants the attention and praise that belongs to God. However, he can only be successful in the lives of those who have not received the gift of grace, salvation, and peace called Jesus Christ. Those who have called on the name of Jesus Christ have the wisdom to recognize satan, the power to fight against him, and the promise of victory over him.

We are the ones who can call forth miracles on earth. We can pray and work to ensure that God's perfect will is accomplished each day. This will happen not by our own strength, but by the power of the Holy Spirit working in our lives. Miracles are God's perfect will manifested. The question is, are you seeking, praying for, and living out God's will for your life and thus allowing heaven to be manifested on earth?

God can do anything, you know—far more than you could ever imagine or guess or request in your wildest dreams! [God] does it not by pushing us around but by working within us, [God's] Spirit deeply and gently within us. (Ephesians 3:20 MSG)

Day 3–Learning from Our Experiences

Earlier in the week, we briefly referenced this truth: most of the time, we get what we expect. Our expectation drives our energy. Meaning, we put our energy into receiving exactly what we expect to receive in life. Oftentimes, our true expectations are hidden in our subconscious mind and we can be unaware of them. It may not be until we recognize certain patterns of behavior that we realize something may be amiss in our thinking. Even when we recognize it, however, we need the Holy Spirit, and sometimes a trained professional, to help us uncover what lies beneath the surface of our thinking and behaving.

Most everyone has heard the phrase, *self-fulfilling prophesy.* Simply put, a self-fulfilling prophesy is a belief that comes to pass because we, knowingly or unknowingly, act as if it is already true. Self-fulfilling prophesies are the reason why many relationships end before they get started. For, if one subconsciously believes that they are only worthy of those who abuse them, they will attract abusers and thus fulfill their initial belief. In the same way, if you believe that you are worthy to be loved by those who are loyal, you will subconsciously attract loyal friends.

Our expectations drive our energy. When we expect something—we put our energy into creating the very thing that we expect, whether we realize it or not. When you look for fault, you will find it. It may take a long time, but eventually you will *uncover* whatever it is that you were looking for all along. When you expect to get hurt by another (mentally, emotionally, or physically), you usually get hurt. When you expect to fail, you fail. The converse is also true. When you expect to be treated well, nine times out of ten, you will be. When you go out looking for honesty, kindness, and peace, you will find them in abundance.

Here is how this can come into play in our faith journey. When we put our faith in Jesus Christ, we are saying that we expect Him to be who He is. Our faith does not make God God. God is. Period. Nevertheless, our faith allows us to see who God is in ways that those who do not exercise their faith never will. You see and you get what you expect. If you expect the Bible to be confusing, contradictory, and false, then when you read it, it will seem confusing, contradictory, and false. Whereas, if you believe that the Bible is the inspired, true word of God, you will read it with a heart of expectation and openness which will allow you to see its truths manifested in, around, and through your life.

Recall and reflect or journal about a time when your expectations about Jesus were met (be specific). What were you hoping that God would do? What were you expecting to do for God? How did the situation unfold? Was your faith strengthened because of this situation?

Meditate upon the following verse asking God to show you any area of your life where you are limiting God because your expectations are negative or too low. Get a picture in your mind of what your life would look like if you exhibited bold faith in Jesus. What is your wildest faith dream? What is keeping you from pursuing it?

Philippians 1:20: For I **fully expect** and hope that I will never be ashamed, but that I will continue to be bold for Christ, as I have been in the past. And I trust that my life will bring honor to Christ, whether I live or die. (NLT, emphasis added)

Day 4—Biblical Character Reflection: Widow in 2 Kings 4:1-7

The book of 2 Kings details the ministry experiences of the prophet Elisha. Elisha is the miracle-working successor to the great prophet Elijah. After receiving the mantel from Elijah, Elisha goes on to perform miracle after miracle on behalf of Jehovah God. In chapter 4 of 2 Kings, Elisha is approached by a widow who is experiencing a serious financial crisis, and in response to her faith, she receives a miracle. Her story is instructive to us because even though she was in a dire and distressing situation, she nonetheless exercised faith and a miracle unfolded.

We can learn a lot from her story, beginning with the fact that it was her *overwhelming obstacle* which made her a candidate for a miracle. Here's the thing: when your situation is the most extreme, the enemy wants you to believe that you have been forgotten and abandoned by God. If we are honest, we feel just that way at times. The key, however, is to have enough faith in Jesus to understand that your obstacle puts you in the "Need a Miracle" line. You cannot get in line to receive a miracle unless and until you first have a need.

When the woman goes to Elisha, he gives her instructions on how to handle her situation. The woman obediently followed Elisha's instructions without asking questions. She had faith to know that Elisha was speaking for God. And, even though what he told her seemed mundane and practical, nonetheless, she obeyed. In fact, Elisha did not give her all the instructions at once, but she was obedient at each step of the way. (See verses 3–5) Develop the discipline to be obedient to the word and instruction of the Lord. You cannot be or experience a miracle if you are not willing to take some faith risks. Things will not always make sense. Things will not always fold or unfold neatly or timely by your schedule. But, your obedience will be rewarded. God is just that type of God.

Another critical component to the woman's miracle is that she had to rely upon *others* for it to come to pass. First, she had to borrow empty vessels from her neighbors, and Elisha was clear that she needed to get a lot of them. Second, she had to go in the house with her sons, shut the door, and act as if she had enough oil to fill all the vessels that she had just borrowed. She did just as she was instructed. Once in the house, her sons started to hand her vessels. She poured the oil and miraculously the oil kept flowing until all the vessels were filled. The oil did not stop flowing until she no longer had the capacity to receive it. She found her miracle!

Banish the notion that God is going to bless you, all by yourself. Miracles rarely happen in isolation. Relationships are too important to God for God not to use other people in the performance of our miracles. You need others and others need you. Interestingly, however, only those who were the closest to the woman observed the miracle as it was happening. All the others were instrumental, but they only learned of the miracle after the fact. Gain the wisdom to know who needs to be with you, behind closed doors, during the crises of your life. There will not be room for everyone. Some people cannot handle observing what God does in secret; they will only be able to hear about it once it becomes public. This means that even you will be on the outside sometimes. Do not be dismayed when this happens. Trust that Christ always does what is right, in your life and in the lives of others.

What else do you see in the story of this widow which led to her receiving a needed miracle?

Days 5-7–Making the Connection. Moving Forward.

Now the One who provides seed for the sower and bread for food will provide and multiply your seed and increase the harvest of your righteousness. (2 Corinthians 9:10 HCSB)

This week we have sought to expand our thinking and expectations about God and what God can do in and through our lives. We have wrestled with the notion that what we expect by faith becomes the framework and, in many ways the limitations, for what we see and experience in life. You should now understand that your faith is a compass which helps to determine where you are and where you are going.

Moreover, your faith should be the barometer for what is going on around you each day. Meaning, if you view life through the lens of your faith, elevating the power and authority of Jesus Christ in every area, you will most likely recognize the miraculous exploits of God that surround you. And, the opposite is true. If you merely take life as it comes, drawing only fear and fact-based conclusions, you will most likely miss, or misinterpret, the hand of God in your life.

The task for us as we move away from this week's study is to stretch our faith to see more of God. Be grandiose, extreme, and deliberate about your expectations from God. Then, live as if you are on your way to receiving exactly what it is that you want and need from God. The more gallant your expectations, the more extravagant and outlandish Christ will be in response. Remember this, God responds to our faith. And, the most important thing about your faith is not that you have it, but the One in whom you have placed it. Jesus makes your faith valuable, not the other way around.

It is also critical to remember that we do not need a lot of faith. We need strong seeds of faith that we are willing to sow into good ground. Jesus was clear that a small seed of faith gives us power to move big things. (See Luke 17:6) Consider sowing more of the following types of seeds as you continue along your faith journey. Sow these seeds in abundance but be careful to sow them in good soil. Be deliberate and intentional. Start at home, and in your own life, then spread them as far and wide as you can. Sow seeds of:

Gratitude. There is a quote seen on social media that simply says, "A grateful heart is a magnet for miracles." When we are grateful, we find ourselves appreciating things and people that others may disregard. Decide to cultivate a spirit of gratitude each day. Then watch as the miracles come into focus. "In every circumstance of life be thankful; for this is God's will in Christ Jesus respecting you." (1 Thessalonians 5:18 WNT)

Generosity. Generosity is about more than just the fact that you give. Generosity is about why, how, and to whom you give as well. Make it a point to view everything that you give, as given to Christ. Remember, that was Jesus' correlation about generosity. He said, "Then the King will answer, 'I tell you the truth, *anything* *you did for even the least of my people here, you also did for me.'"* (Matthew 25:40 NCV, emphasis added) Generosity is its own reward and your generosity may be the miracle that someone else is expecting.

Grace. To plant seeds of grace means to give what is not required or anticipated in each situation. When we are gracious, we set ourselves up to be the recipients and conduits of the best type of blessings—those which surprise us and take our breath away. God is in the business of knocking the wind out of us with God's good, merciful, and grace-filled ways. Grace begets grace. Sow the seeds of what you want to harvest and watch your crops grow.

Using the boat as a pulpit, he addressed his congregation, telling stories. 'What do you make of this? A farmer planted seed. As he scattered the seed, some of it fell on the road, and birds ate it. Some fell in the gravel; it sprouted quickly but didn't put down roots, so when the sun came up it withered just as quickly. Some fell in the weeds; as it came up, it was strangled by the weeds. Some fell on good earth, and produced a harvest beyond his wildest dreams.' (Matthew 13:3–8 MSG)

Week 18–Gratitude
Gratitude Makes the Difference!

Week 18–Gratitude
Gratitude Makes the Difference!

Be thankful in all circumstances, for this is God's will for you who belong to Christ Jesus. (1 Thessalonians 5:18 NLT)

If asked, we would be hard-pressed not to list gratitude as one of the top three most necessary characteristics of any God-follower. That gratitude makes the supreme difference in our lives is both a fundamental and profound truth. Fewer things are more foundational to our faith than gratitude. In fact, even when we lack faith in a certain circumstance, simply being thankful will open our hearts to God. Gratitude calms our fears and gives us mental, emotional, and spiritual strength.

More than just a fundamental need, however, a life of gratitude evidences a deep understanding about the character and personality of Christ. Meaning, learning to remain grateful throughout all the seasons, tests, trials, and circumstances of life helps us to become better acquainted with our Savior. Someone may find that the moment that ingratitude sets in their heart and mind is the very moment that God becomes foggy. However, when gratitude flows freely through your life, you can still trust God, even in those seasons when you cannot trace God.

Think about it. What situation was it that turned your heart from grateful to apathetic? When you stop being thankful, it means that you have ceased to pay attention to who God is and how God is working in your life. Grandma would say that God works in mysterious ways. Well, call it mysterious, nebulous, or just plain confusing; God's ways can be sometimes hard to grasp. But, maybe that is by design. Because, if we could always figure out what God is doing, where would our motivation be to find out who God is?

The fact is that being grateful opens the door to everything beautiful, meaningful, and lasting because gratitude gets us directly to the heart of God. No matter what the situation or who surrounds you in life, gratitude keeps you centered and anchored in the truth. God is always present. God is always powerful. God is always purposeful. God is always worthy of our obedience, praise, and adoration.

This week we will focus on the discipline of gratitude. We will explore what it means to be grateful, not simply as a means of getting more from God, but rather as the methodology for getting more of God. Gratitude is not innate; it is a learned behavior and, believe it or not, ingratitude is learned as well. Let us discover how to cultivate hearts that are grateful, so that all that flows from God's heart can be ours.

Let the peace of Christ rule in your hearts, since as members of one body you were called to peace. And be thankful. (Colossians 3:15 NIV)

Questions to consider: How do you cultivate thankfulness in your life? Is the basis of your relationship with God more about receiving or simply being together? Identify an area of life in which you could be more grateful.

Day 2—Let's Go a Little Deeper

It is good to give thanks to the LORD and to sing praises to Your name, O Most High. (Psalm 92:1 NASB)

Most of us would likely say that we are grateful people who do not mind giving God thanks. In fact, when we hear or read about gratitude, we can mistakenly think that we have already heard everything that there is to know about the subject. We need to fight against this line of thinking, however, because gratitude is one topic to which we can and should return over and over again—daily in fact.

As the psalmist says in the above verse, it is just a good thing to give thanks to the Lord. It is not always logical to be grateful. It is not always easy to be thankful. During tragedy, pain, and disappointment, it feels disingenuous and fake to lift our voices or raise our hands in gratitude. God understands all of that and still we are admonished always to cultivate an attitude of gratitude.

Perhaps God knows that establishing a practice of thankfulness in the everyday calm seasons of life will help us during the difficult times. A friend told me that she once found herself so angry with God that she could not pray, and she did not want to praise. What do you do in those times? First, it is good to recognize that wherever we are and however we may *feel* in the moment, Jesus can handle it. Second, we must remember that gratitude is about trust and faith, not circumstances and emotions. Moreover, gratitude is anchored, not in what God does, but in who God is. We can be grateful when we are rightly related to God. The way to come into right relationship with God is to call on the name of Jesus and receive the gift of salvation offered through His life, death, burial, resurrection, and ascension. So, when we seemingly have nothing else for which we can or want to give thanks, we can always go back to Jesus. Christ's completed work on the cross is a permanent reason to utter thankfulness to God.

What you do in the quiet, mundane, and even monotonous moments of life determines how you will handle the chaos and uncertainty of your moments of calamity. Gratitude makes the most difference in times of crises and confusion. A perspective of gratitude allows us to rise above our current predicaments through reaffirming our faith in the God who transcends time, space, and circumstance. Jesus promises to be with us always. Gratitude brings Christ amazingly close—even in our moments of sin and failure—because it refocuses our attention away from our insufficiency and toward God's great adequacy.

It is interesting to consider, however, that the difficulty most of us have is not in actually *giving* thanks, but rather in being aware of the ways the enemy blocks gratitude in our lives. So, our issue oftentimes is more with managing our ingratitude than with cultivating gratefulness. For that reason, let us look at some ways in which ingratitude can, subtly and without much resistance, slip into our hearts and minds.

Silence/Solitude. We must be alert about what happens in those times when we want to mute our voice and isolate ourselves from God. We all know that there are times and seasons when we must steal away from people and keep quiet about aspects of our lives. God regularly works in those moments. Nevertheless, we should be careful and on guard for those times when we do not want to speak to God and when we act as if we can hide from our heavenly Father. This usually leads to us withdrawing from those to whom we are rightly connected. Moreover, it leaves room for a callousness and hardness of heart to set in. So, just be careful!

Don't give the devil that kind of foothold in your life. (Ephesians 4:27 MSG)

Shame. Unchecked feelings of shame and embarrassment can be a place for ingratitude to rear its ugly head. Whenever you feel inclined to hide and to cover yourself (à la Adam and Eve in Genesis 3:7), you leave yourself open to being bamboozled by the enemy. Shame is simply an indication that we doubt God. God has already made provision for us to get out of the strangest, worst, and most damning of situations. Even when we sin, we do not have to remain in our sinful ways. Acknowledging your sin and confessing your fault gets Christ's attention and brings you back into alignment with God. Do not spend excess time on shame. It serves no good purpose. Instead of shame, shift your energy toward being thankful. Gratitude will remind you that, no matter how bad things are, God is still there and well able to make a way for you. In fact, Jesus is the way that has already been made.

The LORD is near the brokenhearted; He saves those crushed in spirit. Many adversities come to the one who is righteous, but the LORD delivers him from them all. (Psalm 34:18–19 HCSB)

Settling. The spirit to quit is a surefire way to turn our hearts away from thankfulness. Quitting is not the same as resting. We all need times of deliberate rest and relaxation. We quit, however, when we know that we have not completed the task, project, calling, or assignment of God, but we decide to just settle anyway. We have a responsibility to be good stewards over the gifts, talents, and opportunities that Christ has afforded us. When you settle, you essentially say to God—"Thanks, but no thanks."

Jesus said, 'No procrastination. No backward looks. You can't put God's kingdom off till tomorrow. Seize the day.' (Luke 9:62 MSG)

Self-Sufficiency. Self-sufficiency is essentially a refusal to accept what God provides. Anytime we think we can do more or better than God, ingratitude has set in. The beautiful thing about humanity is that we are made in the image and likeness of God, our Creator. This means that intelligence, creativity, and ability are a part of who we are. Never forget, however, that we need God each step along our way. There is no aspect of our lives about which we should not consult with God. Sometimes we are relying on self, and we do not even know it. But, if we are staying connected to God—cultivating intimacy through prayer and study—God will show us the truth. In that very instant, we should repent, yield, and give a shout of thanks!

Trust in the LORD with all your heart, and do not rely on your own understanding (Proverbs 3:5 HCSB)

Day 3—Learning from Our Experiences

Recall and reflect or journal about a time when it was hard or impossible for you to express gratitude to God. Were you focusing more on the circumstance or upon the fact that Jesus was with you in the midst of the trial? Perhaps it was not a trial at all. Have you ever let your elation overshadow and distract you from being grateful? In your mind, is there any difference between giving thanks to God *in* everything and thanking God *for* everything? (Read 1 Thessalonians 5:18)

Meditate upon the following verse considering a time when you may have (even subtly) taken credit for something, as if you did it, instead of giving thanks to God. How did you feel when you realized what you had done? What can you do to guard against that happening again in the future?

Numbers 20:12: *GOD said to Moses and Aaron, 'Because you didn't trust me, didn't treat me with holy reverence in front of the People of Israel, you two aren't going to lead this company into the land that I am giving them.'* (MSG, emphasis added)

Day 4–Biblical Character Reflection: The Leper in Luke 17:11-17

A great example of gratitude making the difference is seen through the life of one leper. The story goes that as Jesus entered a certain village between Samaria and Galilee, He was met by ten men who suffered from a skin disease known as leprosy. The men, being sure to keep the requisite distance as required by law, called out for help. They lifted their voices and asked Jesus to have mercy on them. Here is what Luke records as happening next:

> When he saw them, he told them, 'Show yourselves to the priests.' As they went, they were made **clean**. When one of them saw that he was **healed**, he turned back and praised God in a loud voice. **He quickly bowed at Jesus' feet and thanked him. (The man was a Samaritan.)** Jesus asked, 'Weren't ten men made clean? Where are the other nine? Only this foreigner came back to praise God.' Jesus told the man, 'Get up, and go home! **Your faith has made you well.**' (Luke 17:14–19 GW, emphasis added)

This leper displays a level of gratitude from which we can truly learn. His attitude of gratitude caused him to faithfully display thankfulness to Jesus. Because he had faith and gave thanks, he received something that the other nine men did not get: wholeness. Notice a couple of things about our text. In verse 14, it indicates that as the men went to show themselves to the priest, they were made clean. This word clean in the original Greek language, means to clear or to purify. In verse 15, the text says that one man noticed, not that he had been made clean, but rather, he saw that he was healed. Seeing his healing, he turned back and gave loud exuberant, thanksgiving to Jesus.

This suggests that this man had so much faith that he actually saw himself as completely healed when, in fact, he had merely been cleansed. His faith then caused him to give thanks to Jesus, not for the cleansing, but for the healing. And, after giving thanks for what his faith believed he had received, he got that and more. Verse 19 says that Jesus told him that his faith had made him well. The word "well" (or "whole" in the King James Version) in the original Greek means to save, to deliver, or to protect. So, there are three levels of treatment in our text: cleaned, healed, and made well. There was only one leper who received all three. The difference between him and his nine companions is that he showed gratitude.

We can learn from this leper, not only that being grateful increases our faith, but also that being faith-filled leads us to being grateful. The two work hand in hand. Faith and gratitude feed each other and make our lives better.

What else sticks out to you about this story? Why do you think it was significant to Jesus that the one leper who displayed gratitude was a Samaritan, not an Israelite? Have you ever observed a time when a person who was seemingly an "outsider," perhaps a non-Christian, displayed more faith or gratitude than one who professes belief in Christ? How do you think that makes Jesus feel?

Days 5-7—Making the Connection. Moving Forward.

Soon the people began to complain about their hardship, and the LORD heard everything they said . . . (Numbers 11:1a NLT)

This week we have looked at the impact of gratitude in our lives. It is important to remember not to become lackadaisical about cultivating an attitude of gratitude. As we move away from this topic, consider the story about the children of Israel found in

Numbers chapter 11. It is a precautionary tale for us who want to ensure that we have the proper (grateful) perspective on God and on our circumstances in life. Take a few moments to read the entire chapter, so that you can have context for the following points of emphasis. Correctly evaluated, we can learn at least three things from this story to do to remain thankful.

Be Cautious about Your Company (i.e. External Pressures) (verse 4):

The rabble or riff-raff (as they are called in the Message Bible) were those who tagged along with the Israelites when they left Egypt. These were the ones who lifted their voices in complaint first. It is important to note that they did not know Yahweh, Israel's God. Nevertheless, their bad influence and ungratefulness contaminated the children of Israel and soon they too started to complain loudly to God. We must remember in life that the company we keep is very important. The saying "bad company spoils good morals" is good advice to heed.

The expectations and attitudes of others can cause us to lose sight of just how blessed we are. If we surround ourselves with those who have the wrong mind-set about God, we run the risk of adopting their same mentality. Having an incorrect, or even immature, understanding about who God is, and how God acts, will carry you far away from God. Be cautious about who you allow to speak into your life on a consistent basis. Be careful about from whom you seek guidance and counsel about the situations of your life. You cannot share everything with everybody because their response may not be one of faith, gratitude, or godly wisdom.

It has been said that we can learn a lot about ourselves by simply evaluating the five closest relationships that we have. Who are the people with whom you spend the most time talking and sharing life? God certainly expects us to do life in community. There is no real way to live by faith unless you are meaningfully connected to others who are living by faith as well. Our greatest influence should be the voice of God. Get God's perspective and then make your decisions based upon God's Word and wisdom. Do not let bad company be a source of ingratitude in your life.

Be Careful about Your Cravings (i.e. Internal Pressures) (verses 5–6):

The text indicates that the children of Israel became dissatisfied with what they had because they craved something that they determined to be better. Our appetites and desires need to stay on the things of God and we must be careful that we do not start to dictate to God what is best for our lives. The epitome of ingratitude is when we think that we can provide better for ourselves than God can.

Be careful not to allow the attractive tastes, smells, and colors of the world to cause you to develop disdain for the balanced meals that God serves you freely each day. The children of Israel wanted meat. They remembered the fish, cucumbers, leaks, onions, and garlic that they had for free in Egypt and longed to be filled with those things again.

However, had they forgotten the treachery of Egypt? The meals that they ate in Egypt were, in fact, not free. When we do not watch our cravings, we can find ourselves being lured back to some people, places, and things that may have looked, felt, and sounded good, but were not good for us. When God makes us free, we must retrain our palates so as to not undo our maturity and short circuit our growth.

Whenever you are more focused upon what you do not have, than upon what God is providing for you, be very careful about ingratitude. Unfulfilled desires are a normal part of the natural and Christian life. But, these desires should not have the power or authority to distract us from who God is and all that God has done, is doing, and can do in our lives. Our greatest desire and craving must be for God. Our faith and gratitude will help us to know that God always gives us what is best.

Keep vigilant watch over your heart; that's where life starts. (Proverbs 4:23 MSG)

Be Captivated by What's Common (verses 7–9):

Note that back in Exodus 16, when the manna first fell on the ground, the children of Israel were captivated by it. It was miraculous that God rained down literal bread from heaven. However, in Numbers 11, after they have been eating it for a while, the manna had lost its luster. They were no longer captivated by it but were sick and tired of even the sight of it. The interesting thing, though, is that the manna was still good. They had simply lost the proper perspective about it. It was free. It was tasty. It could be cooked in various ways (boiled or baked). It served its purpose.

We need to be deliberate about remaining captivated by those things (and people) which are easily accessible in our lives. Sometimes, God can bless us so well that we become bored with it, simply because it is free, stress-free, and easy. Think about some of the very blessings for which you wished, hoped, begged, and prayed to God to get. Are you still captivated and enticed by their beauty? Or, has what was once a miracle become simply mundane in your eyes?

Cultivating an attitude of gratefulness will help us to stay captivated by the common blessings that are all around us. The air we breathe, cars we drive, homes we live in— may we never lose our fascination with them. Not to mention our spouses, children, friends, jobs, gifts, and callings—let us stay captivated with it all. Moreover, may we forever be intoxicated with the truth of the love of God, as seen in Jesus Christ our Lord. God, having already given us the best gift ever in Christ, will surely continue to help, protect, bless, and keep us. We must continue to trust the sufficiency of who God is in our lives. Remember, gratitude always makes a big difference.

I will thank the LORD at all times. My mouth will always praise him. (Psalm 34:1 GW)

Week 19–Reconciliation
I Apologize

Week 19—Reconciliation
I Apologize

This is how I want you to conduct yourself in these matters. If you enter your place of worship and, about to make an offering, you suddenly remember a grudge a friend has against you, abandon your offering, leave immediately, go to this friend and make things right. Then and only then, come back and work things out with God.

(Matthew 5:23–24 MSG)

For some people, two of the hardest words to say are "I apologize." People will literally break relationships, stop speaking, or quit coming around, simply because they cannot, or will not, admit that they were wrong. Human vulnerability—a requirement for any apology—is one of the most beautiful sights to behold. Immature human ego is one of the ugliest. Whether we want to believe it or not, it is our ego which keeps us from seeking forgiveness and causes us to avoid being vulnerable. The flesh is a powerful force and, if we are not careful, our flesh will cause us to dishonor God.

God is relational. And, healthy, dynamic, and authentic relationships are very important to God. When we are in right relationship with our sisters and brothers, God is honored and pleased. One thing that we all know to be true is that humans are prone to make mistakes. It is a part of our very nature. No one is perfect, and perfection should be expected from no one. Nevertheless, we tend to be very hard on ourselves, and especially hard on others, when they prove to be what we all are—human. Why is this?

Perhaps it is because not apologizing, breaking relationship, and being disconnected is easier than we would like to admit. That is not to say that we are casual or nonchalant about our relationships because most of us are not. But, another truth which is less easy to admit, but no less valid, is that sticking together, admitting our wrongs, walking in love, and being reconciled is hard work.

Reconciliation sounds easy sometimes when we read about it in the Bible or when preachers preach about it from the pulpit. But, we have all tried and know the truth. Humanity—with all our fickle, fainthearted, and fake ways—is not easy to love. In fact, one of the reasons why we are witnessing some of the strife, pain, and incomprehensible acts in our day and time is because we are finding it extremely hard to first love ourselves, which then makes it pretty much impossible to love others. Therefore, it does not matter if you are the offender or the offended in any given situation; we need Jesus to help us. We do not have it within ourselves to maintain God-honoring and healthy relationships. Part of the reason is because the enemy fiercely opposes such relationships. The devil is gleeful whenever he can spark distrust, disillusionment, and even disdain between individuals. The heart of God is delighted when we walk in agreement, extend grace, and forgive others of their faults and failures. We can do all of this by the grace of God.

This week, we will study the topic of reconciliation, seeking to uncover the heart of God for resolving conflict and healing relationships. We will develop strategies for how to stay in, and avoid falling out of, relationship with others. We will learn to be better witnesses for Christ in the world.

So now I am giving you a new commandment: Love each other. Just as I have loved you, you should love each other. ***Your love for one another will prove to the world that you are my disciples.*** (John 13:34–35 NLT, emphasis added)

Questions to consider: Have you ever experienced a broken relationship with someone because of an offense? Is reconciliation even a remote possibility in that relationship? Has anyone ever broken relationship with you because they refused to acknowledge and apologize for a wrong? How did that make you feel? Have you ever been the one who did not apologize? What led you to make that decision?

Day 2—Let's Go a Little Deeper

We are therefore Christ's ambassadors, as though God were making [God's] appeal through us. We implore you on Christ's behalf: Be reconciled to God. (2 Corinthians 5:20 NIV)

At its heart, apologizing is about reconciliation. Being reconciled is no small feat. Once an offense occurs one must go through a series of steps to decide if reconciliation is desired and possible. We can agree that reconciliation on the natural, human level is only made possible because of what God has done for us spiritually. Earlier in 2 Corinthians 5, Paul says that our salvation

> "is from God, who reconciled us to [God] through Christ and gave us the ministry of reconciliation: That is, in Christ, God was reconciling the world to [God], not counting their trespasses against them, and [God] has committed the message of reconciliation to us." (Verses 18–19 HCSB)

It is important that we catch the sequence of how things are supposed to flow; otherwise, we will be working to no avail, like one attempting to fill a bucket that has a hole. Being in right relationship with God is a gift that was secured for us by Jesus on the cross. Once we receive this gift, we have the ability to be in right relationship with others. It is our relationship with Christ that puts us in the proper position to have healthy relationships with other people. We cannot truly have one without the other.

Therefore, when you are offended and considering if you can be reconciled with the other person, you should imagine that Christ is the One who will do the reconciling through you. You will not be required to do this work for yourself, but rather you must allow Christ to do it though you. Your job is simply not to block or hinder the work of the Holy Spirit in the process. When you fully submit to the power of Christ—through humility and obedience—then the Holy Spirit will be able to work. If the other party is willing to do the same, reconciliation is possible. That reconciled relationship can then be an example of what Christ can do through the yielded lives of Christ's disciples.

When we understand how God ordained for relationships to work, we can start to appreciate why apologizing is so important to healthy relationships. **Reconciliation requires an acknowledgment of wrong.** Before we can join with God, we must acknowledge that we need a Savior and accept the work of Jesus Christ on Calvary's cross as our very own. In other words, there must be repentance. We see calls for repentance all throughout the gospels and the Acts of the Apostles. Moreover, repentance is not merely saying you were wrong. It is also admitting that you need to change and agreeing to come into relationship with Christ so that change can be made.

Similarly, in our human relationships, reconciliation requires some type of acknowledgment and repentance. Understand this: we can forgive without an apology. We can pray for our sister or brother who has offended and hurt us without receiving an apology. But, we cannot be fully reconciled to someone who has not acknowledged and apologized for their wrong. Neither does God ask us to do so. One place where we can miss the heart and mind of God is by thinking that God is okay when we disregard and overlook an offense. Not so. When at all possible, God wants offenses to be confronted and resolved, so that God's children can walk together in unity, peace, and love. (See Matthew 18:15–17) We cannot carry out the ministry of reconciliation that has been assigned to us if we misapprehend how that ministry is intended to flow.

Another point which may be obvious, but should still be stated, is that someone who has not reconciled and accepted the salvation offered by God cannot truly be reconciled to another human. This does not mean that we cannot be friends, coworkers, and confidants, etc., with those who do not share our faith. But, it does mean that we should not hold them to the same standards that we hold other believers because they have never agreed to those terms. They have never asked the Lord to help them and, as stated earlier, reconciliation is a work that requires the wisdom, grace, and strength of God.

Unmet expectations are a huge reason why relationships of all kinds deteriorate. Do not take Christian standards into your relationship with a non-Christian. There is no way that they can ever meet those expectations. Christians cannot even maintain those standards without the help of the Holy Spirit, so how could a non-believer? God expects us to be God-honoring in our relationships and yet we know that every relationship is not equal. So, it is healthy to exercise wisdom and discretion.

Consider yourself. How do you handle it when you hurt someone's feelings? Are you healthy enough to acknowledge your wrong, repent, and seek forgiveness? If this is difficult for you, know that you are not alone. Remember that God loves you perfectly and will not abandon you or banish you from the family because you do not do this well. Understand however, the Holy Spirit will not allow you to remain where you are. That nudging in your spirit and that sinking feeling in your stomach is likely God trying to get your attention. It is time to grow up.

So let me say it again, this truth: It's better for you that I leave. If I don't leave, the Friend won't come. But if I go, I'll send him to you. When he comes, he'll expose the error of the godless world's view of sin, righteousness, and judgment: He'll show them that their refusal to believe in me is their basic sin; that righteousness comes from above, where I am with the Father, out of their sight and control; that judgment takes place as the ruler of this godless world is brought to trial and convicted. (John 16:7–11 MSG)

Day 3—Learning from Our Experiences

Recall and reflect or journal about a time when you had to give an apology. Did you do it quickly? How did it feel to offer an apology? What about a time when someone offended you? Were they aware that they hurt you? How did it make you feel to confront them? Did they apologize? Has the relationship been reconciled?

Meditate upon the following verses while prayerfully asking God to show you any relationships in your life that need reconciliation. Did the other person offend you or did you offend them? Are they a believer of Jesus Christ? Is reconciliation a possibility from your perspective? Why or why not?

Matthew 18:15–17: If a fellow believer hurts you, go and tell him—work it out between the two of you. If he listens, you've made a friend. If he won't listen, take one or two others along so that the presence of witnesses will keep things honest, and try again. If he still won't listen, tell the church. If he won't listen to the church, you'll have to start over from scratch, confront him with the need for repentance, and offer again God's forgiving love. (MSG)

Day 4—Biblical Character Reflection: Paul, in Writing to Philemon

That is why I am boldly asking a favor of you. I could demand it in the name of Christ because it is the right thing for you to do. But because of our love, I prefer simply to ask you. Consider this as a request from me—Paul, an old man and now also a prisoner for the sake of Christ Jesus. (Philemon 1:8–9 NLT)

In the Letter of Philemon, the apostle Paul models for us the true power and authority that fellow believers have in setting relationships right among Christians. The entire letter is a mere twenty-five verses, so it would be good for you to take a few moments to read it before continuing, so that you can follow along.

The brief background is that Onesimus is a slave owned by Philemon. At some point, Onesimus ran away from his duty as a slave and became acquainted with Paul. During the time that the two of them were together, Onesimus converted and became a fellow believer in Jesus Christ. Now, Paul is sending him back home to Philemon. This letter is Paul's plea that Onesimus be received back on good terms; not as a slave, but as a brother, a Christian, as if he were Paul's representative.

Paul displays three important characteristics as he practically seeks to carry out the ministry of reconciliation between Philemon and Onesimus. He shows affection, authority, and appeals a Christian's need to fully align with the heart of Christ. These are the same characteristics that we should seek to display when given the opportunity to facilitate reconciliation and the restoration of broken relationships in our own lives, in our churches and families, and beyond.

Affection (verses 1, 5, 7, 16): The foundation of all relationships is love. Love comes in different forms, but some level of love must be applied to all relationships, if they will be healthy. In this letter, Paul draws upon the love that Philemon has for Christ and other believers, and the friendship that the two of them share. Paul encourages Philemon to receive Onesimus, not as a runaway slave, but rather, as a dearly beloved child of Paul and brother in Christ.

When we are seeking to be reconciled in our own relationships or to help facilitate reconciliation between others, let us start with love. Mutual affection can fade, but if handled properly, it can also be rekindled. The space between brokenness and healing takes a process to overcome. Nevertheless, God's grace and the shared bonds of love, which connect us, can make reconciliation attainable. Let love lead the way.

Authority (verses 8, 9, 14, 17, 19, 23): Paul takes an interesting approach in dealing with a very sensitive issue with Philemon. He does not command him outright to receive Onesimus back. Rather, he appeals to his own authority as an elder, a prisoner of Christ Jesus, and the one by whom Philemon was converted, to request that the right thing be done. Moreover, Paul writes this letter, not only to Philemon, but also to Apphia, Archippus, and the entire house church that Philemon leads. By doing this, Paul highlights the fact that believers have a responsibility to one another to uphold the standards and example of Christ in our relationships.

Perhaps, if Paul had simply demanded that Philemon did what was right, he would have ended up hijacking the means to get to his desired (and appropriate) end. We can learn from his approach that our end and our means must be congruent. God will not send us to do the right thing in the wrong way. When we come in the power and the authority of Jesus Christ, He gives us the boldness, compassion, wisdom, and grace to do right and to be right. Authority is a powerful tool when it is wielded with love and anchored in grace. Outside of that, authority can destroy that which it has been set in place to preserve.

Alignment (verses 11, 16, 20, 25): The final way that Paul appeals to Philemon to be reconciled with his brother is by asking him to align with the word and will of Christ. Paul uses the word "brother" multiple times in this short passage. By doing this, he draws attention to the fact that because Onesimus is now "in Christ," he is a new creation. (See 1 Corinthians 5:17) When Onesimus ran away, he was a slave, literally the personal property of Philemon, according to the laws and customs of the day.

But now, upon his voluntary return, Onesimus is a brother, a believer, a son of Paul, and a friend. Paul expects Philemon to treat this brother the way he would treat Paul the next time he came. The way Paul goes about things also ensures that the proper standard can be applied to other individuals as well, not just to Onesimus. The issue was truly bigger than Philemon and Onesimus anyway. It was about how one human treated another, especially another who was also a fellow believer in Jesus Christ. By appealing to Philemon to do what is right in the eyes and heart of God, Paul left room for him to proactively be reconciled to many others.

Most of the time, people want to do the right thing. We want to be connected to one another properly and to walk in wholeness. Sometimes, we just need to be gently reminded of the standard of Christ. The truth is, when we allow reconciliation to happen through us, all we are doing is giving to others that which we have already received from God. We cannot fail when we align ourselves with our heavenly Father. God promises to help us, protect us, and heal us when we seek to put God first.

But God shows [God's] great love for us in this way: Christ died for us while we were still sinners . . . While we were God's enemies, [God] made friends with us through the death of [God's] Son. Surely, now that we are [God's] friends, [God] will save us through [God's] Son's life. (Romans 5:8 and 10 NCV)

Days 5-7—Making the Connection. Moving Forward.

When I was a child, I spoke like a child, I thought like a child, I reasoned like a child; when I became an adult, I put an end to childish ways. (1 Corinthians 13:11 NRSV)

Matters of the heart (romantic and otherwise) can be a hairy road to navigate. Most of us would not have a problem being and staying in relationship with others, if people only knew how to act. It is okay to say amen right there! Furthermore, our flaws are only magnified the more time we spend in one another's company. So, even though with time some things do become more natural, time is no substitute for attention, alertness, kindness, and tenderness. In fact, the longer you know people, the more, not less, you will be expected to invest in keeping that relationship vibrant and fresh.

Another reason, in addition to the behavior of others, why relationships can be difficult, is our own sense of inadequacy. Some people self-sabotage and avoid connecting with others because they feel so unworthy. Others simply know that we have a limited capacity or tolerance for the frailties of others, so we would rather not deal with what we call "the drama."

Well, no matter where you fall on the continuum, whether you are the one who easily cultivates relationships, you must be poked and prodded to be in relationships, or you are somewhere in the middle, the truth is we all need these connections just the same. We are in that same boat together.

Therefore, this is the perspective on relationships that should be our guide moving forward: relationships are the best and only way for us to truly know God and to know ourselves. In fact, we cannot live a true life of faith absent meaningful connections with others. Living faith in a vacuum is not truly living by faith at all. In all honesty, it is impossible to know yourself, unless and until you link up with the right people with whom you can live authentically. God designed life to be lived in relationship, not out of it.

The Christian faith is not about religious dos and don'ts; but rather, what distinguishes our faith is the relationship we are offered with God through faith in Jesus Christ— God's only begotten Son. Jesus is our anchor in relationships. Jesus is our reference point when offenses and disagreements occur. Jesus is our source of strength, peace, love, joy, hope, determination, and perseverance when it comes to being rightly related to God and others. As we move away from this topic, consider these three things that we can do as we seek to be in relationship and be reconciled to those from whom we sometimes drift apart.

Expect **Divine Intervention.** One of the best things we can do for our relationships—present and future—is expect God to help us in them. When you are going through good times and in those times when offenses and sensitivity abound, remember that Jesus is interested in your relationships. God cares about you and God cares about the quality of the relationships that you have with others. Our job is to make room for divine intervention. Trust that God is able and willing to help you to build and sustain healthy relationships.

Be open to healing; be available to restoration; and be willing to forgive. None of this can be done by mere human strength. It takes godly wisdom and supernatural strength to bear with some people and to get through some situations. Do not put more pressure upon yourself than you can handle. Allow for time and space when necessary. God can often work better in our silence than through our words and actions. Let God orchestrate and guide you along every step of your relationship journey. Listen for God's voice. Watch for God's hand to move. God is a mender of brokenness and God is a healing balm. Trust and believe.

Now to him who by the power at work within us is able to accomplish abundantly far more than all we can ask or imagine. (Ephesians 3:20 NRSV)

Embrace actions that **Defy Intelligence.** In our relationships, sometimes the illogical, seemingly unintelligent thing, is the right thing to do. This may mean waiting when you want to push ahead. It may mean showing tough love now because you know that in the long run it will be what is best. God always operates in realms that are beyond us. Yet, in God's mercy and because of grace, we can get a glimpse of what God is doing when we seek God earnestly. Nevertheless, seeing God always requires faith. After all, if we could figure it out without faith, we would not need God. But, faith is not smarts. Godly wisdom does not act the same as worldly wisdom. So, sometimes we must be willing to act in ways that defy our human intelligence, but that line up perfectly with the word and will of God.

Consider some biblical counsel on the matter:

Let no one be under any illusion over this. If any man among you thinks himself one of the world's clever ones, let him discard his cleverness that he may learn to be truly wise. For this world's cleverness is stupidity to God. It is written: "He catches the wise in their own craftiness." And again: "The Lord knows the thoughts of the wise, that they are futile." (1 Corinthians 3:18–20 Phillips NT)

Woe to those who are wise in their own eyes and clever in their own sight. (Isaiah 5:21 NIV)

Exhibit a **Determined Insistence.** If our relationships are going to succeed, we cannot quit on them. This is not a statement intended to diminish the real, harsh, gut-wrenching issues that can arise when we are seeking to walk out life with another person. But, the truth is, the only way we will make it is if we simply do not give up. We must keep pushing through. Keep laying the groundwork for wholeness by exhibiting strength and sincerity each day.

Determined insistence means not getting stuck in the actual things people may do when you know that their intention was right. Deal with the behavior and move on. Oftentimes, our neglect of the issues can become a bigger problem than the issues themselves. We look up and realize that we have been separated so long that the fact of the separation is now much bigger than the reason why we broke up. Being determined does not mean that one party gets to prescribe to the other what reconciliation, healing, or growth looks like. We can only control ourselves. Sometimes we should just allow our loved one to struggle and work a thing out in their own way and time. It is not a formula. It is a determined insistence to not walk away, or at least not to stay away forever. It is a decision to persevere, press, maintain, and endure because you know that God is with you and you know that God will help you.

Always be humble and gentle. Be patient with each other, making allowance for each other's faults because of your love. Make every effort to keep yourselves united in the Spirit, binding yourselves together with peace. (Ephesians 4:2–3 NLT)

Week 20–Fear
Don't Be Afraid!

Week 20—Fear
Don't Be Afraid!

The LORD is my light and my salvation; whom shall I fear?
The LORD is the strength of my life; of whom shall I be afraid?
(Psalm 27:1 NKJV)

Perhaps one of the most pervasive and persistent enemies with which we must contend in this life is fear. Fear comes in many shapes and forms. Yet, no matter how it comes, fear does not play fair. The most unconscionable thing about fear is that it misrepresents reality and manipulates our senses. Fear causes you to respond and react in ways that are not only unnecessary, but also not reasonable, even for the circumstances as they are presented. But, the thing is, fear does not present circumstances properly. So, you must know that when you listen to fear, you will get the story all wrong.

For example, fear tells us that what is possible with God is totally impossible. Fear persuades us to believe that what we know, see, and understand is all that there is to a matter. The truth is, however, there is always more to the situations and circumstances that we experience. More than we see. More than we know. More than we can understand. Fear can cause us to act rashly, even in the face of real danger and uncertainty. Sure, we must admit that there are times in life when being afraid is warranted. The ability to recognize and avoid danger is a good thing.

Nevertheless, being paralyzed, perplexed, and imprisoned by fear is not God's desire for your life. That kind of fear does not come from God. Fear that causes us to think and act irrationally is a weapon used by the enemy to steal our joy and make us forget our authority in Christ. Remember, "God has not given us a spirit of fearfulness, but one of power, love and sound judgment." (2 Timothy 1:7 HCSB) No matter how substantial the obstacle we are facing may be, it is not greater than God. God is victorious, and we are yet more than conquerors through Christ. (See Romans 8:37) Fear is a liar. Fear misconstrues. Fear cannot be trusted. Do not succumb to fear. Do not be afraid.

The only way to guard against having unhealthy fear is by the power of God's Holy Spirit. God does not want us to live in fear of the known or unknown circumstances that we may face. God wants us to mature and develop as spiritual beings, so that when we are afraid we will know to come to Christ straightway. Jesus is our keeper, provider, and protector. As we learn to understand the power and ability of Christ better, fear will subside. We can depend on God to take care of us. We do not need to believe the bad reports of fear. This week we will study fear with the aim of learning how to detect when it is present and to better know when, and how, to ignore or heed its warnings.

For God did not give us a spirit of timidity (of cowardice, of craven and cringing and fawning fear), but [God has given us a spirit] of power and of love and of calm and well-balanced mind and discipline and self-control. (2 Timothy 1:7 AMP)

Questions to consider: What do you fear? Is your greatest fear of something that is known to you, or do you fear the unknown? How do you seek to manage your fears in your daily life? Have you ever overcome a fear? How did you do it?

Day 2–Let's Go a Little Deeper

I am leaving you with a gift—peace of mind and heart. And the peace I give is a gift the world cannot give. So don't be troubled or afraid. (John 14:27 NLT)

The secret to not being managed—or mismanaged—by fear is to remember the great authority that you have as a child of God, and more specifically, as a follower of Jesus Christ. The gift of peace, which Jesus gives us, is our strongest defense against fear. The trouble is, however, that peace seems to escape us when we need it the most. Why is this? Perhaps it is because we do not truly understand or know how to use this wonderful gift.

We need to approach peace the same way that we handle a longed-for electronic or kitchen gadget that we have gotten for Christmas. First, we need to get excited about the fact that we have peace. And, second, we need to figure out how to use it correctly. For, the more that we understand it, the more natural it will become for us to *let* our hearts rest in peace. (See John 14:1)

We can be excited about peace for several reasons. Most importantly, Jesus gives it to us and He considers it a wonderful gift. All throughout the New Testament, Jesus granted peace to those whom He encountered. Peace is a blessing that comes from being connected to God through Jesus Christ. Peace is one of the many rewards that comes to us from trusting God, believing in Jesus, and standing on the Word of God. When you think about the fact that you have peace, it should cause your heart to leap for joy!

Yet, simply knowing that we have peace is not enough. We must learn to use peace each moment of our lives. One way to do this is to *allow* peace to rest upon us. Do not resist peace, welcome it. When you feel fearful, fretful, or fainthearted, pause and ask God to fill you with peace. In that moment, your mind can be diverted away from your problem and toward God's presence. God's presence is the source of peace. God is eternal and abides with us continuously, therefore we have direct access to peace.

So, when for whatever reason, you are troubled and disturbed, experience the gift of peace by refocusing and becoming aware of God's presence. Do this by simply pausing and taking a deep breath. Or, refocus by reading and reciting a biblical promise that applies to your current situation. Press into peace by singing a praise song or meditating on the words of your favorite hymn. Resist fear, worry, and doubt by letting the gift of peace come to the forefront of your heart and mind. No matter what you may be facing, God has already gone before you, God goes with you, and God surrounds you. You are protected, provision is available, and peace from Jesus Christ is yours. Grab it!

So do not fear, for I am with you; do not be dismayed, for I am your God. I will strengthen you and help you; I will uphold you with my righteous right hand . . . For I am the LORD your God who takes hold of your right hand and says to you, 'Do not fear; I will help you.' (Isaiah 41: 10, 13 NIV)

Day 3—Learning from Our Experiences

Recall and reflect or journal about a time when you were filled with fear. Why were you afraid? Did you feel alone or abandoned? Or, were you troubled because the outcome was uncertain? How did you handle your fear? Were you able to let your heart be at peace even before the situation was resolved? What did you learn about God through that experience? What did you learn about yourself?

Meditate upon the following verses asking God to give you a new and deeper understanding about the sufficiency of God's presence. Reflect on a time when God sheltered and covered you— before, during, or after a trial or difficulty. Purpose in your heart to remember the truth that "Jesus Christ is the same yesterday, today, and forever." (Hebrews 13:8 NLT) Since Jesus does not change, you can trust His abiding presence to be with you and to keep you each moment of every day. You do not need to be afraid.

Isaiah 43:2–3a, 5a: When you pass through the waters, I will be with you; and when you pass through the rivers, they will not sweep over you. When you walk through the fire, you will not be burned; the flames will not set you ablaze. For I am the Lord your God, the Holy One of Israel, your Savior . . . Do not be afraid, for I am with you. (NIV)

Day 4—Biblical Character Reflection: Rahab in Joshua 2

You have likely heard the saying that "faith and fear cannot exist in the same place at the same time." It seems like a logical conclusion. Nevertheless, many of us have found that the opposite of this statement is true. Faith and fear are two sides of the same coin. In life, those of us who have put our faith in Jesus will indeed have to face our fears to overcome our problems. We cannot wait for fear to pass us by, no we must do some things, even while we are afraid.

A biblical example of this is seen in the life of a woman named Rahab. We are introduced to Rahab's story in Joshua chapter 2 and it concludes in chapter 6. Take some time to read these chapters today. Here is a quick summary of the story. Rahab lived in the city of Jericho and two Israelite spies came to her house as they were investigating the city. When the king of Jericho learned that the spies were at Rahab's house, he sent orders for her to release the men. Instead, Rahab hid the two men and told the king's men that the spies had fled. Later, Rahab went to talk to the spies in the place where they were hiding. She admitted to them that she and all of Jericho were deathly afraid because of the impending doom of their town. But, rather than cower to her fear and remain silent and distressed, Rahab spoke up.

Rahab asked the men to guarantee that she and her entire family would be kept alive and safe when Jericho was eventually conquered. Amazingly, the two men granted her request. Later, when Jericho was overthrown, the men remembered their promise, and Rahab, and her family that was with her, were taken out safely. Rahab's story is instructive for us because it shows that when we confront and face our fears, we can gain strength, peace, and protection from God and others.

One very interesting thing about Rahab's story is that she was apparently motivated to hide the spies and to ask for their future protection because of what she had heard about their God. During her conversation with the men, Rahab says that the main reason that the people of Jericho are so afraid is because they have heard the testimony of what the God of Israel has done in the past. It is her understanding about the power and faithfulness of God that caused Rahab to declare, "The Lord your God is the supreme God of the heavens above and the earth below." (Joshua 2:11 NLT) Rahab was afraid, but she still had faith to believe that this supreme God would (through these spies) grant her and her family the peace and protection that they needed.

Rahab's story teaches us that our faith in God can overcome our belief and understanding about our current predicaments, if we will be courageous and operate in wisdom. What else about Rahab's story stands out to you? How do you think you would have responded had you been in Rahab's shoes? Have you ever had to make a stand of faith, even though you were afraid?

Joshua said to the two men who had spied out the land, 'Go into the prostitute's house and bring her out and all who belong to her, in accordance with your oath to her.' So, the young men who had done the spying went in and brought out Rahab, her father and mother, her brothers and sisters and all who belonged to her. They brought out her entire family and put them in a place outside the camp of Israel. (Joshua 6:22–23 NIV)

Days 5-7–Making the Connection. Moving Forward.

Earlier in the week, we referenced John 14:27. Look at the verse again: "I am leaving you with a gift—peace of mind and heart. And the peace I give is a gift the world cannot give. So don't be troubled or afraid." Notice that Christ gives us the gift of peace both for our mind and for our heart. Jesus did not want to leave any room for us to fall into the hands of fear. So, Christ's peace covers the two aspects of the human makeup that are most inclined to be afraid—the heart and mind. Let us break down exactly what this means for us practically.

The thing that we must come to understand is that our mind and our heart learn and respond differently, even to the same situation. Our mind tends to want empirical, scientific, or hard evidence before it will yield to peace. Whereas our heart can be comforted by the mere memory of what God has done or the expectation of what God can do. Our mind wants something tangible, whereas the heart can be satisfied with words.

Peace for the Heart. We set the expectation of our heart, and determine what it will remember, by what we allow to flow into it. For the heart absorbs whatever we allow it to have in abundance. So, if you continually allow toxic, fearful, and stressful people and things to get close to your heart, your heart will be full of toxins, fear, and stress. On the other hand, if you drench your life with praise for God, gratitude, promises of peace, and positivity, such will be the character of your heart. And, like a magnet your heart will be drawn to what is a match for it and repelled by whatever is not a good fit. So, while your heart can be easily injured, the good news is that your heart is also resilient and can respond quickly to the healing grace of Jesus. Keep guarding your heart! (See Proverbs 4:23)

Peace for the Mind. The mind is altogether different. The mind is suspicious and regularly draws conclusions that are based upon its limited understanding and experience. The mind does not simply absorb what you put around it. The mind is set by intentionality and once set it does not easily change. Have you ever met someone who has a made-up mind about something and no matter what you say or do, they cannot be swayed? Many people feel this way about God or coming to church. They think they already know all that there is to know, simply based upon their experiences.

So, even if that person is confronted with testimonies and biblical passages to the contrary, they will nevertheless hang on to what they have seen and experienced. They can even be told that their experiences, even though real, are not the standard or norm. But, unless they want to change their minds, they will not. A mind that is fixed can either be a thing of beauty or a total disaster, it all depends upon on what it is set.

For believers, we should fix our minds on the character, reputation, and words of God. If we do this, we will trust God's sovereign power and protection, despite tangible indications that God cannot be trusted. Contrarily, if fear gets set in a mind, it can be very difficult for it to be dislodged. This is one reason why the apostle Paul instructs us to "be transformed by the renewing of your mind." (Romans 12:2a) Paul understood that only renewing the mind (continuously setting it according to God's Word and truth) would allow us to live life successfully.

As we prepare to leave this topic, consider the following ways that you can tangibly and practically cultivate peace in both your heart and your mind:

Embrace Change. Overcoming fear will require change. Fear is most often a learned response and the way to dispel it is to change how you think or interact with whatever makes you fearful. Change is rarely immediate, but it is possible by the power of God. If you have an area, relationship, or situation in your life that continues to cause you fear, consider what you can change about it, so that you can experience God's peace. If you stay the same, it does not matter what happens in that situation because eventually you will end up at the same place all over again. However, if you change—allow God to strengthen you, mature you, and give you wisdom—the situation will have less power and authority in your life. Change is always an option; embrace it.

New wine calls for new wineskins . . . (Mark 2:22 NLT)

Be Courageous. Courage is the ability to forge ahead even though you recognize that you will face danger and difficulty. Many times, fear keeps us in bondage because we do not have the courage to step up and step out. What we must remember is that when we act courageously, we are not alone. God is with us as we pursue our hopes and dreams. God will stay with us no matter what the forecast or terrain is up ahead. The road to our purpose and destiny will not always be smooth. Nevertheless, whatever you must overcome along the way will be worth it when you see the end that God has planned. *Be Courageous!*

Haven't I commanded you? Strength! Courage! Don't be timid; don't get discouraged. God, your God, is with you every step you take. (Joshua 1:9 MSG)

Be Consistent. Once you embrace change and choose to be courageous, you must keep at it, even when you want to turn back. If you will overcome your fears and achieve the change that you seek in life, you must be consistent. You must be willing to get up each time that you fall and to persevere when you would rather quit. God can help you to experience peace as you consistently make choices that honor and put God first. Sometimes in life, we are afraid because we know that the consequences of our actions warrant punishment. We cannot remove our ability to make mistakes. Nonetheless, we can avoid some mistakes altogether by fortifying our hearts and minds through faithful obedience to God. Try to take God at God's word in a new way today. Get up tomorrow and do the same thing again and again. Be consistent!

Above all, be strong and courageous to carefully observe the whole instruction My servant Moses commanded you. Do not turn from it to the right or the left, so that you will have success wherever you go. (Joshua 1:7 HCSB)

Order Information

REDEMPTION
P R E S S IP

To order additional copies of this book, please visit
www.redemption-press.com.
Also available on Amazon.com and BarnesandNoble.com
Or by calling toll free 1-844-2REDEEM.

CPSIA information can be obtained
at www.ICGtesting.com
Printed in the USA
BVHW031949191119
564296BV00001B/50/P